GLOBETROTTER™

Travel Guide

MOROCCO

D1079866

ROBIN GAULDIE

NEW
HOLLAND

NEW
HOLLAND

★★★ Highly recommended
★★ Recommended
★ See if you can

Third edition published in 2008
by New Holland Publishers (UK) Ltd
London • Cape Town • Sydney • Auckland
10 9 8 7 6 5 4 3 2 1

website: www.newhollandpublishers.com

Garfield House, 86 Edgware Road
London W2 2EA, United Kingdom

80 McKenzie Street
Cape Town 8001, South Africa

Unit 1, 66 Gibbes Street,
Chatswood, NSW 2067, Australia

218 Lake Road, Northcote,
Auckland, New Zealand

Distributed in the USA by
The Globe Pequot Press, Connecticut

ISBN 978 1 84773 095 4

Publishing Manager: Thea Grobbelaar
DTP Cartographic Manager: Genené Hart
Editors: Carla Zietsman, Alicha van Reenen, Sean Fraser
Picture Researchers: Shavonne Govender, Colleen
Abrahams
Design and DTP: Nicole Bannister, Lellyn Creamer
Cartographers: Genené Hart, Tanja Spinola, Elaine Fick
Consultant: Sue Bryant

Reproduction by Resolution (Cape Town) and Hirt & Carter
(Pty) Ltd, Cape Town.
Printed and bound by Times Offset (M) Sdn. Bhd.,
Malaysia.

Acknowledgments:
Robin Gauldie wishes to thank GB Airways and Meridien
Hotels for their help in researching the book.

This guidebook has been written by independent authors
and updaters. The information therein represents their
impartial opinion, and neither they nor the publishers
accept payment in return for including in the book or
writing more favourable reviews of any of the establish-
ments. Whilst every effort has been made to ensure that
this guidebook is as accurate and up to date as possible,
please be aware that the facts quoted are subject to
change, particularly the price of food, transport and
accommodation. The Publisher accepts no responsibility
or liability for any loss, injury or inconvenience incurred
by readers or travellers using this guide.

Keep us Current
Information in travel guides is apt to change, which is
why we regularly update our guides. We'd be grateful to
receive feedback if you've noted something we should
include in our updates. If you have new information,
please share it with us by writing to the Publishing
Manager, Globetrotter, at the office nearest to you
(addresses on this page). The most significant contribution
to each new edition will receive a free copy of the
updated guide.

Dedication:
The author would like to dedicate this book to the memory
of author, journalist and photographer Ann Jousiffe.

Photographic Credits:
Todd Brown: page 63; Mary Duncan: page 103; FF/Patricia
Aithie: pages 9, 76, 97; FF/Mike Fitchett: pages 71, 84, 93;
FF/M. Hannaford: pages 11, 114; FF/Bob Pearson: pages 44,
50; GI/Glen Allison: page 24; GI/Thomas Dressler: pages
15, 21; GI/Jason Laure: pages 16, 17, 19; GI/Penny
Tweedie: page 18; Philip Game: page 36; Robin Gauldie:
pages 6, 7, 8, 10, 20, 27, 28, 29, 30, 31, 32, 33, 34, 51, 56,
59, 61, 62, 64, 70, 99, 101, 108, 110, 115, 116, 117, 118,
119, 126; HL: page 45; HL/Jeremy Horner: page 87; HL/P.
Moszynski: page 47; Ann and Peter Jousiffe: pages 41, 52;
Fiona Nichols: title page, pages 4, 14, 23, 48, 66, 67, 68,
79, 112; Christine Osborne: page 96; IPB/Jeanetta Baker:
pages 25, 86, 90; IPB/Peter Baker: cover, pages 12, 22, 35,
72, 81, 82, 85, 94, 102; TI/David Forman: page 13; TI/Ken
Gibson: page 39; TI/Guy Marks: pages 73, 98; TI/Kevin Nicol:
page 105.
[FF = fotograff; GI = Gallo Images; HL = Hutchison
Library; IPB = International PhotoBank, TI = Travel Ink]

Cover: *Hassan II Mosque, Casablanca.*
Title Page: *Camels are a popular form of transport.*

CONTENTS

1
Introducing
Morocco

Exotic yet accessible, Morocco is a land of teeming medieval bazaars and tiny mountain villages, palatial hotels and simple inns. Glowing landscapes stretch from snowcapped mountain ranges to fertile lemon groves and vineyards, from desert sand dunes to beaches kissed by the Mediterranean or swept by the surf of the Atlantic.

This is a land crammed with surprises. Fashionable boutique hotels stand tucked away in the crowded streets of centuries-old market districts or among the battlements of fortified villages. Cool, palm-shaded terraces beside turquoise, tiled swimming pools look out over red and pink mountains and the spires of minarets. Sophisticated restaurants, serving some of the finest food in the world, await behind carved wooden doors guarded by doormen in the baggy white trousers, pointed leather slippers and embroidered waistcoats of medieval retainers.

Fashionably exotic in the 1950s and 1960s, Morocco at the beginning of the 21st century is being rediscovered by the glitterati. Its dazzling African light and its colours – the rose pink of medieval palace walls, the mellow ochre-red of old mud-brick kasbah walls and the bright blue of the sky over the High Atlas – are a photographer's delight. Many cultures meet in this westernmost outpost of the Muslim world, which is also the closest of all Arab nations to western Europe.

Very much part of the **Arab** world, Morocco has also been much influenced by **Europe** and sub-Saharan Africa.

TOP ATTRACTIONS

*** **Djemaa el-Fna:** jugglers, pedlars, food stalls and fire eaters in Marrakech.
*** **Drâa Valley:** from the Atlas mountains to the Sahara.
*** **Dadès Valley:** miniature castles and palmeries along the Kasbah Trail.
*** **Essaouira:** medieval battlements, picturesque streets and Atlantic beaches.
*** **The Fez Medina:** the most fascinating of all Morocco's many medinas.
** **Roman Volubilis:** Ruins of an ancient empire.

Opposite: *Colourful textiles and rush baskets are among the most typical souvenirs of Morocco.*

FACT FILE

Area: 710,850km² (274,460 sq miles)
Population: 27.5 million
Capital: Rabat
Second city: Casablanca
Highest mountain: Jebel Toubkal (4167m/13,670ft)
Longest river: Oued Drâa (1100km/680 miles)
Official language: Arabic
Official religion: Islam
Currency: Moroccan dirham (100 centimes).

Below: *In the cedar forests of the high Moyen Atlas, snow can occur from November to March.*

On a clear day, Tangier – its most northern town – lies within sight of Gibraltar and the southern tip of Spain, only 15km (9 miles) away, while Guelmin, in the deep south, was once the terminus for camel caravans trekking through the desert wastes of the Western Sahara to the great African entrepôt of Timbuktu.

Many **Moroccan cities** are really two towns in one, with a modern ville nouvelle built during the French colonial era surrounding the mud-brick walls, minarets and narrow alleys of a much more picturesque and typically Arab old town. In the **new town**, with its straight, tree-lined boulevards, shops and pavement cafés and bars, you could be forgiven for thinking you might be in some French provincial town. Inside the walls of the **old souk**, however, you enter an entirely different world of crammed alleys, men in the traditional nightshirt-like djellaba, veiled women, and hawkers and craftsmen plying their age-old trades, where mint tea is favoured over liquor, and a bag of illicit hashish, or kif, may be on sale. Major cities such as Rabat and

Casablanca are modern and partly Europeanized, but in walled villages high in the snowcapped Atlas mountains the 21st century has yet to make much of an impact on a traditional way of life. On the coast, the solid ramparts of fortified fishing ports like Essaouira and Ksar es Seghir hark back to a time when the Barbary corsairs sailed these waters, menacing merchant ships and shore settlements alike.

Morocco's climate and terrain show as many extremes as its culture. In winter, heavy snow may fall on the peaks of the Atlas while oranges ripen and jasmine blooms in the more temperate lowlands of the north, and the sun blazes down on the sand dunes of the south.

Hardly a stone's throw from Europe, this is a land that has much to offer the visitor: a mellow year-round climate and fine beaches, striking and varied scenery, and a fascinating culture influenced not only by the Arab world but by a strong native Berber culture, by medieval and modern Europe, and by sub-Saharan Africa.

Above: *Palm trees and clover fields in the green and fertile Tinerhir oasis lie within sight of the arid, treeless slopes of the Moyen Atlas.*

THE LAND

To Arabic speakers, this long, thin country on North Africa's Atlantic coast is *al-Maghreb al Aqsa* – 'the land furthest west, in the setting sun'. The **Atlas Mountains**, rising to summits of more than 3000m (10,000ft), form a natural rampart between Morocco and its eastern neighbour, Algeria.

The country has around 600km (370 miles) of **Mediterranean coastline** between Tangier, where the Mediterranean meets the Atlantic, and Saidia, on the Algerian border. Much longer is its **Atlantic coast**, stretching for approximately 2500km (1555 miles) from Tangier to Nouadhibou and the border with southern neighbour, Mauritania.

Between the Atlantic and the Atlas ranges lie fertile lowlands where date palms, citrus, cotton and sugar cane grow. Cool, moist winds from the Atlantic temper the North African heat, giving Morocco a **mellow climate** for much of the year.

LARGEST CITIES

Casablanca: population 3,070,000
Rabat/Salé: population 1,230,000
Fez: population 750,000
Marrakech: population 500,000+
Meknès: population 500,000
Oujda: population 500,000
Agadir: population 500,000

Above: *The ancient medina of Fez, huddled around the Kairaouine Mosque, is one of the world's oldest continuously inhabited medieval settlements.*

The Cities

Morocco's major cities include **Tangier**, on the Mediterranean coast; **Casablanca**, the French colonial capital and the centre of most of the country's industry and business; and **Rabat**, the modern royal capital and seat of government. All three settlements blend modern influences with traditional Moroccan lifestyles. Perhaps even more fascinating are the imperial cities of **Fez**, **Meknès** and **Marrakech**, founded by Islamic emirs more than a thousand years ago and rich in mosques, palaces, fortifications and bazaars. In the walled kasbah villages of the southern Atlas, an even more traditional way of life continues.

Rabat, the country's capital since independence in 1956, lies on the Atlantic coast, 278km (175 miles) south of Tangier, and has gradually expanded to virtually incorporate the seaside city of Salé, just to the north, with almost no open country between the two. Casablanca, Morocco's largest city, biggest port and most important commercial and industrial centre, is also on the Atlantic coast, just under 100km (62 miles) south of Rabat.

The heart of any Moroccan community, no matter how small, is the souk, or **marketplace**. In the great historic cities, such as Fez and Marrakech, this may be a virtual city within a city, with hundreds of tiny shops and open-air stalls selling every conceivable product and service. In smaller towns, the market is held once a week in an open square where villagers and peasants gather to buy and sell. They bring mounds of fruit and vegetables, herbs, cheeses and spices. Purple turnips, vivid orange carrots, vermilion tomatoes and great golden pumpkins make a colourful display, while around the market square are the workshops of village **artisans** – cobblers, knife grinders, tailors and furniture makers. Many of the villagers and smallholders arrive by donkey cart, especially in the Rif and Atlas mountain communities where modern tractors are outnumbered 10 to one by mules drawing wooden ploughs. Much of the fruit and vegetables is organically grown, as many small farmers cannot afford costly pesticides and chemical fertilizers, and the produce is very different from the symmetrical version familiar to Western shoppers. Tomatoes, for example, are rarely perfectly spherical. Butchers' stalls, on the other hand, can be less appetizing, with gobbets of meat and offal piled in the open air, sometimes under a swarm of flies.

The Coast

Much of Morocco's **Atlantic** coastline is one long beach, swept by fine Atlantic rollers and backed by sand dunes. Surprisingly, little of this coastline is developed for tourism, but there are clusters of resort hotels around Tangier, between Casablanca and Rabat, and at Agadir, the purpose-built resort city in the south, some 510km (315 miles) south of Casablanca. Essaouira, an attractive historic port 350km (215 miles) south of Casablanca, has also become a chic place to visit for fashion-conscious Europeans. South of Agadir, the coast is almost completely undeveloped, though **fine beaches** skirt a string of small towns such as Ifni, Plage Blanche, Tan Tan Plage, Tarfaya, Laâyoune Plage, Boujdour, Ad-Dakhla and Nouadhibou. Few of these have any facilities for tourists, with only basic accommodation and simple local restaurants.

The Mountains

Two mountain ranges dominate northern and central Morocco. Parallel to the Mediterranean coast, the verdant **Rif mountains** rise to heights of 2200m (7220ft). A stronghold of the Berber clans, these mountain ranges were the heartland

WHITE WATER

The rivers of the High Atlas flow fastest in early spring when they are fed by melting snow from the high peaks. The longest whitewater descents include the 145km (90-mile) trip down the **Oued Ahanesal** and **Oued Melloul** in the Atlas, while the 60km (37-mile) **Oum er-Rbia** is navigable all year. For information, contact the **Royal Moroccan Federation of Canoeing**, National Sports Centre, Avenue Ibnou Sina, BP 332 Rabat, tel/fax: (03) 777 0281.

Below: *Atlantic breakers sweep the Moroccan coast near Casablanca, Morocco's main seaport.*

Opposite: *Though the landscape looks barren, Berber shepherds find pasture for their sheep on the slopes of the Middle Atlas.*
Below: *Oasis pool, palm trees and barren mountains in the Drâa Valley.*

of resistance to French and Spanish colonialism and are still somewhat lawless to this day, being the main area of cannabis cultivation.

At its eastern end, the Rif chain merges with the **Atlas**, a 1200km (745 miles) sierra that separates coastal Morocco from the Sahara. With many summits topping 2000m (6550 ft), the Atlas peaks out at 4167m (13,670ft) at **Jebel Toubkal**, the highest peak in North Africa, which is clearly visible from Marrakech. The Atlas is subdivided into three sections: the **Moyen (Middle) Atlas**, running between the Mediterranean coast and the fertile plains just north of Marrakech; the **Haut (High Atlas)**, which rise from foothills on the Atlantic coast near Agadir to form a crescent overlapping at its northeast end with the eastern slopes of the Moyen Atlas; and the **Anti Atlas**, a third crescent of peaks between the southern High Atlas and the eastern plains and valleys fringing the Sahara Desert.

Morocco's major **rivers** rise in the snows of these three ranges and flow most strongly in spring, when they are fed by melting snow and seasonal rains. The **Moulouya**, rising on the slopes of Jebel Ayachi, flows north to the Mediterranean and forms a man-made lake behind the Mohammed V Dam, north of Taourirt. The **Sebou** rises in the Moyen Atlas to flow into the Atlantic near Rabat, while the **Rbia** also rises in the Moyen Atlas and meets the ocean near El-Jadida. Rising in the High Atlas, the **Ziz**

and **Dadès** rivers flow through dramatic gorges to water the plains and valleys of the east before dying in the Sahara, while the **Drâa**, Morocco's longest river, flows through another spectacular valley before looping south across the Algerian border, then back out of the desert and into Morocco again to flow into the Atlantic at Cap Drâa, just north of Tan Tan.

The Steppe, Desert Fringes and Deep South

The valleys and plains to the east of the Atlas ranges, watered by rivers and smaller streams, are often surprisingly lush, but less than 150km (95 miles) away lies the Algerian border and the true Sahara of the **Grand Erg Occidental** (the Great

Western Waste). Between this more fertile zone and the desert proper lie regions of tussock grassland unique to Morocco and sometimes called the **Moroccan steppe**, traditional homeland of pastoral Berber horsemen and their flocks of sheep and goats. South of Guelmin, at the southern end of the High Atlas, the land becomes

HISTORICAL CALENDAR

2nd century BC to 3rd century AD Rome rules Mauretania Tingitana.
3rd–7th centuries AD North Africa divided among Berber tribes and Vandal invaders.
683 First Muslim Arab invasion.
703 Second Muslim invasion, conversion of Berbers to Islam.
788 Idris I establishes the Idrissid dynasty.
9th century Idrissid realm expands.
1062–1213 Emergence and expansion of the Almoravid empire.
Mid-13th to late 14th century Merenid dynasty based in Fez.
1415–97 Portugal seizes Mediterranean and Atlantic ports, Spain expels Moors from Al-Andalus (Andalucia) and takes Melilla.
1472–1549 Wattasid dynasty rules from Fez.

1510–74 Saadian dynasty conquers all of Morocco, then overthrown by Ottomans.
1578 Portuguese defeat at Battle of Three Kings leads to peace treaty.
1578–1603 Reign of Ahmed al-Mansour followed by anarchy.
1664–72 Moulay Rachid founds Alaouite dynasty.
1672–1727 The reign of Moulay Ismail.
1832 France bombards Essaouira.
1844 French incursion into Morocco.
1859 Spain seizes Tetouan.
1907 French occupation.
1941–43 Morocco governed by French Vichy government in collaboration with Nazi Germany.
1943 Morocco 'liberated' by Free French forces.

1956 France hands over power to Sultan Mohammed V (1956–61). Morocco gains independence.
1972 Hassan II introduces first Moroccan constitution.
1975 Hassan II leads Green March into Western (Spanish) Sahara. Spain withdraws from Western Sahara.
1975–2001 Polisario movement resists Moroccan rule in Western Sahara.
1993 Majlis an Nuwab (Chamber of Representatives) founded.
1997 Bicameral legislature established.
2000 The death of Hassan II and the succession of Mohammed VI.
2002 First multi-party elections held.
2004 Free trade agreement with USA.

Above: *Homes made of pisé (red clay brick) in a typical Berber village in the Ziz valley.*

increasingly **arid** and barren until, south of the Drâa, the **desert** begins in earnest in a region of dunes (erg) and pebbly plateau (hammada) stretching south to the border with Mauritania.

Southern Morocco, also called **Western Sahara**, is sparsely populated, though rich in mineral resources, and the government has tried to encourage more settlement in the region with ambitious irrigation and agricultural development schemes.

Climate

Morocco's climate is influenced by the **Atlantic**, which brings cool, moist winds in winter and sea mist to the southern coast even in summer. Most of the country has four distinct **seasons** – a short, cool, wet winter; a short, warm spring (March to April); and a long, hot summer ending with a short, dry autumn. In Tangier, the climate is **Mediterranean**, with temperatures reaching a high of around 35°C (95°F) in mid-summer and falling as low as 15°C (59°F) in winter. Further south, maximum temperatures can climb to more than 40°C (74°F) in the **Sahara**, plummeting close to freezing at night.

Those visiting the southern resort city of Agadir in search of guaranteed winter sun may be disappointed, as rain is a possibility there throughout the winter – as it is throughout northern and central Morocco.

However, hot summer sunshine is guaranteed from April onward. For most visitors planning a

TANGIER	J	F	M	A	M	J	J	A	S	O	N	D
MAX TEMP. °C	16	16	17	18	24	25	27	27	26	22	18	17
MIN TEMP. °C	8	8	9	11	16	17	18	18	16	15	11	9
MAX TEMP. °F	61	61	63	64	75	77	81	81	79	72	64	63
MIN TEMP. °F	46	46	48	52	61	63	64	64	61	59	52	48
HOURS OF SUN DAILY	6	7	8	9	11	12	12	12	12	12	8	7
RAINFALL mm	52	52	53	40	25	5	0	0	8	25	40	40
RAINFALL in	2.5	2.5	2.5	2	1	0.2	0	0	0.3	1	2	2
DAYS OF RAINFALL	15	15	20	10	8	1	0	0	2	10	10	12

holiday that combines poolside or beach sunbathing with active exploring and sightseeing, the best times to visit are May–June and September–October.

Fauna

With a striking range of environments and ecosystems, Morocco has a wide variety of wild animal species. There are more than 30 national parks and nature reserves, ranging from **Tamri**, an area of coastal cliffs and lagoons near Essaouira, to **Toubkal**, surrounding the highest peak in North Africa, and **Iriqui**, on the edge of the Sahara.

The large **wild animals** that were once found here – including the Barbary lion, leopard and some varieties of desert antelope – have all been hunted to extinction, and desertification and deforestation through poor agricultural practice threatens many more, with no less than 30 species on the endangered list.

Smaller **mammals** abound, and there is rich bird life. In the foothills and mountains, wild boar, mongoose, monkeys (including the so-called 'Barbary ape' – actually a species of macaque), Barbary sheep, pine marten, red fox and genet are among the more striking mammal species, along with a wide range of rodents and bat species. Otters are found along mountain streams and rivers. The desert fringes, and the desert itself, have a surprisingly rich fauna, including the fennec (or bat-eared

SURFING SPOTS

Windsurfers head for **Essaouira** and **Taghazout**, discovered by French wind-surfers and with great winds, waves and simple places to stay and eat. Around Essaouira, spots such as **Sidi Kaouki** offer perfect wind-surfing conditions, with waves between 0.5m (1.5ft) and 2.5m (8ft) high, water temperature of about 20°C (68°F) and Force 4–7 winds. At Taghazout, there's beginner-level windsurfing at the main beach and more demanding conditions 1km (0.5 mile) south, at points nicknamed **Anchor**, **Mystery** and **Killer**. For surfing and windsurfing information, contact the Royal Moroccan Surfing Federation, tel: (022) 25 95 30, fax: (022) 23 63 85.

Below: *Flamingoes wade in coastal wetlands in the Massa National Park near Agadir.*

SUFIS AND SAINTS

Muslim holy men, or *walis*,
are venerated by many
Moroccans – especially in
rural Berber regions, where
their tombs are places of
pilgrimage and worship –
and are known as *marabouts*.
Many of these 'saints' – such
as the 8th-century **Moulay
Idriss**, whose tomb is in the
town named after him – were
members of the mystical Sufi
(or dervish) sects that prolifer-
ated across the Islamic world
over the centuries, and are
regarded with suspicion
by the more orthodox
Muslim authorities.

Below: *Wheatfields near
Fez, in one of the coun-
try's most fertile farming
regions, are overlooked
by the Middle Atlas.*

fox), golden jackal, Dorcas gazelle and the jerboa, or
desert rat, as well as the striped hyena, the rare and
endangered addax antelope and the edmi gazelle.
Reptile species include the common chameleon, spiny-
tailed lizard, Berber skink, horned viper and horseshoe
snake, as well as the common gecko, seen at night on
walls and ceilings of older buildings, especially near
lights that attract the insects on which it preys. More
than 300 resident and migrant **bird species** have been
recorded. In spring and autumn, Morocco is a cross-
roads for migrant birds, including cranes, storks and
raptors such as the osprey.

Endemic to Morocco is the endangered bald ibis.
Other rare species to be seen include Levaillant's
woodpecker, Moussier's redstart, Audouin's gull and
Eleanora's falcon, found on the rocky islets off Essaouira.
Merja Zegra, a coastal lagoon north of Rabat, is a fine
location for ducks, geese, waders and flamingoes, while
Tamri, south of Essaouira, is the most likely spot to see
the bald ibis. The higher mountains are the haunt of
larger **raptors** such as the lammergeyer, with its 3m
(10ft) wingspan, while three species of bustard – the
great, little and the very rare houbara bustard – may be
found in the grass-
lands fringing the
Sahara.

Insect life is equally
rich. Among the most
evident insect species
is a variety of colourful
butterflies, including
the vivid yellow
cleopatra, the large
African swallowtail,
scarlet cardinal, mar-
bled white, painted
lady, red admiral and
a number of species of
blue, including the
Larquin's blue.

Plant Life

Despite deforestation, Morocco still has rich **woodlands** both in the lower plains and hills and in the higher ranges. Native vegetation includes cork oak and a unique wild pear found only in the Mamora forest between Rabat and Meknès. Holm oak, cedar and wild olive, along with several species of pine and fir, grow thickly on the Rif mountainsides and in the foothills of the Atlas, giving way to juniper and dwarf pine on the higher slopes.

The Atlas is extremely colourful in spring, with **wild flowers** including peony, poppy, orchid species, geranium, viburnum, and scarlet dianthus turning slopes and forest glades into explosions of crimson, bright yellow, purple and violet. Endemic to Morocco is the argane tree, which once grew in extensive forests but is now at risk from goats, forest fires and replanting with commercial timber such as pine and eucalyptus.

HISTORY IN BRIEF

The first traces of human habitation in North Africa date from around 17,000 years ago, while more recent remnants of early humankind in the region include rock drawings near Akka, in the Anti Atlas. Little is, in fact, known of the people of the region until the advent of

Above: *Poplar plantations and cornfields provide a stark contrast to the grim red desert cliffs and slopes which surround the Dadès Valley.*

BALD IBIS

Fewer than 200 breeding pairs of bald ibis survive in the wild, with populations restricted to a handful of breeding sites that include the lagoons and cliffs at **Tamri** on Morocco's Atlantic coast. Once widespread in Europe, the bird has suffered from habitat depletion around the Mediterranean and is now found only in Morocco and Turkey.

Above: Islam's holy law prohibits representational art, so Moroccan artisans have elevated calligraphy and abstract geometric decoration to a high level.

the **Phoenicians**, the great traders of the Mediterranean, whose ships sailed from what is now Lebanon to Spain and even as far as the British Isles. By the 8th century BC, they had established themselves in **Carthage** (in modern Tunisia), with bases on the Moroccan coast at Tingis (Tangier) and Mogador (Essaouira).

By the 4th century BC, Carthage was the greatest power in the Western Mediterranean, but in the 3rd and 2nd centuries BC, the mighty Carthage clashed with Rome – the region's other great power – and was defeated. It was entirely destroyed in 146BC.

The **Romans** called the North African hinterland Mauretania (not to be confused with the modern republic of Mauritania), but Rome had very little real impact until 33BC, when the local ruler, King Bocchus II, died, leaving his kingdom to Rome. Bocchus's kingdom was divided into two. His possessions in what is now Algeria became **Mauretania Caesariensis**. Morocco became known as **Mauretania Tingitana**, and the former Carthaginian colony at Tingis became its capital. Rome's hold was loose, never stretching much further than the coast, and by the 3rd century AD, the Empire maintained only a foothold in Tingis. When the Roman Empire in western Europe collapsed in the early 5th century AD, North Africa was settled by Teutonic barbarian peoples, the **Visigoths** and the **Vandals**, who had migrated toward the south through the Iberian Peninsula in search of new lands. They ruled the region until 533AD, when they were ousted by a renewed Roman (or Byzantine) Empire based at **Constantinople** (modern Istanbul). The clans and chieftains of the mountains, plains and deserts of Morocco were hardly affected by these events.

IMAMS AND MUEZZINS

Islam has no priests, but the weekly sermon is read by an *imam*, or religious scholar, who must be well versed in both the Koran and the *sharia*, the code of Islamic law. The call to prayer is the responsibility of the *muezzin*, who traditionally had to climb a steep spiral stairway to the top of the minaret. These days, the faithful are summoned by a pre-recorded call broadcast by loudspeakers, and all the *muezzin* has to do is switch on the cassette player.

The Advent of Islam

A new power was, however, sweeping across the Middle East and North Africa. Born in far-off **Arabia** in the 7th century AD, the Islamic faith found immediate converts among the Arab peoples. The green flag of the **Prophet Mohammed** and his successors was carried from Arabia, through Egypt and across the desert, sweeping away Byzantine rule in North Africa by 689AD. The conquest and conversion of Morocco were delayed by squabbles over the succession to the **caliphate** (leadership of the Islamic world) and by resistance from the indigenous **Berber people** of the region, but by 710 the Emir Musa bin Nusayr had established control over most of the country, his success due more to persuasion than conquest, with the Berbers gradually accepting Islam and its leaders. Morocco, along with all of what is now Tunisia, northern Algeria and parts of Libya, became the emirate of **Ifriqiya**, subject to the Ommayad caliph of the whole Islamic world, whose capital was Cairo in Egypt.

> **RAS AL-HANUT**
>
> This typical Moroccan **spice mix** has up to 20 ingredients, including dried rose petals. To make a simple but authentic version, finely grind three cinnamon sticks with a pestle and mortar and blend with two teaspoons of ground turmeric, one teaspoon of ground black pepper, half a teaspoon of freshly grated nutmeg, half a teaspoon of freshly ground cardamom seeds, and half a teaspoon of ground cloves. If stored in an airtight container, the mixture will keep its flavour for up to two months.

The Heyday of the Moors

The Maghreb quickly became Islam's bridge to the conquest of Christendom. Berber converts provided Musa and his generals with foot soldiers and horsemen, and they seemed invincible, rolling over Spain and deep into France before finally meeting defeat at the hands of the Frankish Emperor **Charlemagne** at Poitiers in 732. For the next seven centuries, the Iberian peninsula remained mostly in the hands of the '**Moors**', as the descendants of these Maghrebi conquerors were known to Europeans.

Moorish cities such as Granada and Cordoba enjoyed a golden age of commerce, learning and creativity, and **Al-Andalus**, as Moorish Spain was once called, had close links with the Maghreb.

Below: *Fantasias, in which horsemen dressed in the robes and head-dress of Berber raiders gallop by firing volleys of musketry, are now only seen at tourist resorts, and are a pale imitation of the real thing.*

IBN BATUTA

Born in Tangier in 1302, Ibn Batuta is the Arab world's Marco Polo. Setting out on the pilgrimage to Mecca after completing his studies as a scholar of Islamic law, he spent the next 25 years travelling throughout the Islamic world and beyond, all the way to the East Indies and even to China. Returning to Morocco in 1354, he left an account of his travels in Asia before setting off again, first to West Africa and then to Spain. He died in 1377.

Below: *Desert nomads with their camels near Erfoud, on the fringes of the Sahara Desert.*

In the Maghreb

Back in Morocco, where Berbers were increasingly treated as second-class citizens by the Arab Ommayad caliphs and their emirs (regional governors), resentment turned into revolt in 739 when the Berber garrison of Tangier mutinied, sparking a nationwide rising. During the following three years, Berber armies drove the Arabs across the Atlas range and came close to conquering Tunis, encouraged by missionaries of the doctrinaire **Kharijite** sect of Islam, a purist group whose preaching of racial equality was welcomed by the Berbers. By the mid-8th century, Berber-Kharijite states under elected imams had been established around Tafilalt oasis in southern Morocco and at Berghouata, south of Rabat. The rest of Morocco relapsed into a patchwork of tribal lands and merchant cities.

The Idrissids

From this chaos emerged a series of dynasties founded by dynamic leaders. In 788, a rebel Arab prince, **Idriss bin Abdullah**, arrived in Morocco as a refugee after picking the losing side in the struggle for the caliphate between two great Islamic dynasties (the victor was the great Caliph Harun al Rashid, who moved the capital of Islam to Baghdad). Idriss became leader of a confederation of Berber tribes, but was assassinated by one of Harun's agents in 791. His son, **Idriss II**, nevertheless went on to build a new city at **Fez**, where he reestablished orthodox Islam and, through war and diplomacy, founded a dynasty that, by the time of his death in 828, loosely controlled most of northern Morocco. On his death, his lands were divided between his own sons, and Idrissid princes ruled in Fez until 923.

The Ommayads and Fatimids

The Ommayad dynasties of Moorish Spain and the Fatimids of Tunisia vied for control of North Africa throughout the 10th century. The leaders of each claimed to be Caliph of all Islam, and the entire Maghreb was drawn into the struggle. In 917, the Fatimid ruler **Baydalla Said** conquered northern Morocco – from the

Mediterranean coast as far south as Fez – only to be driven out a few months later by the Ommayad leader **Abdul Rahman III**.

By the mid-10th century, the Ommayads controlled most of Morocco, mainly through alliances with local rulers, but by 979 the Fatimids had driven them back to a few footholds on the Mediterranean coast. By the end of the 10th century, the dynastic struggle had finally run out of steam, and the Fatimids eventually succeeded in conquering Cairo, centre of the Islamic world, losing interest in trying to take Morocco. The Ommayad kingdom in Al-Andalus eventually fell apart after Abdul Rahman's death in 976 and the succession of his 10-year-old son, **Hisham III**.

The Almoravids

In 1062 a new force emerged when the Koranic preacher **Abdallah bin Yasin** forged an alliance of **Saharan Berbers**, known for their religious teachings as 'the people of the monastery' (al-murabitin, or Almoravids). Making Marrakech their capital, the Almoravids conquered territory stretching from the lands south of the Sahara to as far north as Saragossa in Spain. Though their roots were in the purist Islamic tradition that runs strongly through the history of the

Above: *Royal guards dressed in traditional costume parade outside the royal palace at Rabat.*

WARRIOR MONKS

The **Almoravids** came from the deep south of the Maghreb, in what is now Mauretania, where two Muslim preachers founded a *ribat*, or warrior monastery, which became the nucleus of a holy war to propagate a pure form of Islam. Before turning north to the fleshpots of Morocco, they had already destroyed the ancient, pagan African empire of Ghana in the southern Sahara.

Above: *Marabout Sidi Aissa shrine, one of many monuments to Muslim holy men venerated throughout Morocco.*

medieval Maghreb, the Almoravids apparently succumbed to the pleasures of the flesh, ignoring Islam's stricter prohibitions, and were in turn overthrown by an even more conservative group, known as the Al-Muwahhidin ('proclaimers of the unity of God') or Almohads. Led first by Mohammed Ibn Tumart (1080–1130), then by Abd al-Mu'min (Abdel Moumen) between 1139 and 1163, they conquered the entire Almoravid Empire by 1147 and, by 1159, had established an empire that covered over most of North Africa. Under Abd al-Mu'min's successors, notably his younger son Abu Yacoub Yusuf (1163–84) and his son Yacoub al-Mansour (1184–99), Almohad power continued to grow, and in 1203 – under Mohammed an Nasir (1199–1213) – the Almohad empire reached its peak with the conquest of the Balearic Islands. On the death of Mohammed an Nasir, however, tribal leaders and local princes once again began to break away, and the last of the Almohads, Ishaq, was to rule over only the tiny principality of Tinmal in the Atlas, conquered by a new rising power in 1276.

The Merenids
Abou Yahya (1245–58), leader of the **Beni Merin** – largest of the Berber tribes of eastern Morocco, moved into the power vacuum left by the decline of the Almohads, and created a new empire with its capital at Fez, where he built a new seat of government outside the original city walls. He and his successors were, however, unable to reconquer the Tunisian and Algerian territory once ruled by the Almohads.

The Reconquista

By the 15th century, the Moorish emirates of Iberia were in decline and the kingdoms of Portugal, Castile and Aragon began to test their strength. In 1415, Portugal seized Ceuta and, in 1457, they took Ksar es Seghir. Tangier fell in 1471 and over the next two decades they seized harbours down the Atlantic coast, including Asilah, Larache, Azemmour and Mogador. **Portuguese** successes contributed to the unpopularity of the last Merenid sultan, **Abdul Haq** (1418–65), who was eventually overthrown and killed in a rising led by religious scholars in 1465.

From 1469 to 1492, following the marriage of **King Ferdinand** of Aragon to **Queen Isabella** of Castile, their united kingdoms campaigned against the Moorish emirs, forcing the last emir of Granada to surrender in 1492. From around 1480, those Muslims (and Jews) who were able flee Spain for the Maghreb began to do so, and the flow eventually became a flood after the Reconquista (reconquest) exposed them to the full intolerance of **Spanish Christianity**. In 1497, Melilla fell to Spain and, in the early 16th century, the Maghreb appeared to be vulnerable to full-scale invasion. Spain, however, was

THE SAHARA

The Sahara Desert, which borders Morocco to the east and south, is the **world's largest**, measuring some 1600km (1000 miles) from north to south and around 5150km (3200 miles) from east to west, covering almost 9.1 million square kilometres (3.5 million square miles). With the rise of Islam and the Arab conquest of North Africa, trade across the desert increased, reaching its height in the 13th–16th centuries when **caravans** linked Moroccan ports such as Essaouira and Agadir with the medieval African empires of Somngkai, Ghana (nowhere near the modern state of that name), Bornu, and Kano.

Below: *Where the Drâa Valley ends, the dunes of the Sahara Desert start.*

unable to do more than establish strongpoints on the North African coast, and was soon evicted from even these, eventually retaining only **Ceuta** (which it acquired from Portugal) and **Melilla**.

The Wattasids

While their Arab neighbours to the east (in what are now Tunisia and Algeria) became vassals of the **Ottoman Empire** and were drawn into its struggle with Spain, the Moroccan rulers found **Portugal** a greater threat. Following the overthrow of Abdul Haq, his former kingdom was ruled by a council of religious leaders until 1472 when **Mohammed al-Sheikh**, emir of Asilah, retook the city and founded his own dynasty, known as the Wattasids. The Wattasid sultans controlled central Morocco, including Meknès, Fez and Rabat, but their power gradually waned and, despite alliances with the Ottoman Empire, they were usurped by yet another new dynasty, the Saadians, whose power base was in the Drâa Valley.

The Saadians

The first of the Saadians, **Mohammed al-Qaim** (1510–17) rose to power as elected leader of a federation of southern tribes. His sons, **al-Araj** (1517–40) and **Mohammed al-Sheikh** (1540–57), resisted the Portuguese and, in four decades of war, conquered the whole of Morocco. The Saadians took Marrakech in 1525, drove the Portuguese out of Agadir in 1541, and took Fez from the Wattasids in 1549, before pushing across the Atlas to invade the territories of the Ottoman Empire in Tunisia. Though pushed back by the Ottomans, the Saadians extended their power to the north, where **Sultan Abdulah al-Ghalib** (1557–74) conquered

Below: *The modern ceremonial gateway to the centuries-old Royal Palace at Fez.*

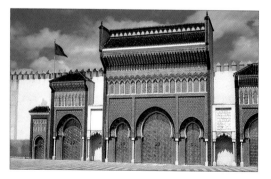

Chefchaouen (where the last of Idrissi sultans had hung on since the 1450s) in 1562.

Al-Ghalib's successor, Mohammed al-Muttawakil, was deposed by an invading Ottoman Turkish army, which replaced him with puppet sultan Abdul Malik (1567–68). In 1578, Al-Muttawakil tempted Portugal into an alliance and a Portuguese army of 25,000 marched on Fez from the coast. The **Battle of the Three Kings** ended, however, in the annihilation of the Portuguese and all three kings – Mohammed, his rival Abdul Malik, and the young Portuguese Dom Sebastian – died in the battle. The Portuguese eventually abandoned their Atlantic ports, and Abdul Malik's younger brother Ahmed – later called **Al-Mansour** (the Victorious) – became sultan (1578–1603). His reign was peaceful and prosperous, benefiting from peace with Portugal and a rebuilding of trade across the Sahara, with a Moroccan garrison occupying the gold trade centre of Timbuktu. When he died, however, a three-way war broke out between his sons, ruining the country, destroying the Saharan gold trade and putting an end to his dynasty. Yet again, Morocco became an assortment of mini-states, ruled by warlords, religious leaders or elected councils. There were even pirate republics, such as Salee (Salé), founded by refugees from the Andalucian cities conquered by Spain.

The Alaouites

Following half a century of chaos rose the man whose descendants rule Morocco to this day – **Moulay Rachid** (1664-72), founder of the Alaouite dynasty. Leading a group of tribes from the eastern plains, Rachid captured Fez in 1666 and Marrakech in 1668 and, in a series of

Above: *Roman mosaic at Volubilis, once capital of Mauretania Tingitana.*

HASH AND KIF

Cannabis indica, or hemp, has long been a staple crop in Morocco, and hashish – the solid resin of the plant – is still smuggled from the Rif mountains across the Straits to Spain and thence all over Europe. Until recently, local people were allowed to grow **hemp**, as few other crops could be cultivated. In theory, the entire crop was bought and destroyed by the government each year. In practice, only a fraction of the harvest was handed over by the growers – and not all of that was destroyed by the police. Efforts to curb the trade centre on encouraging villagers to grow alternative crops, but it is hard to find an equally profitable substitute. Hashish and *kif* (the finely chopped leaves of the plant) are widely sold in Morocco, especially in the Rif, but are **illegal**.

whirlwind campaigns, had complete control of Morocco by the time of his death in a riding accident in 1672. His younger brother, **Moulay Ishmael** (1672–1727), presided over an era of prosperity, defeating several revolts with an army of African slave warriors, and forcing the Spanish and Portuguese out of several of their remaining coastal forts. On his death, strife between his many sons once again led to anarchy, and his successors **Moulay Abdullah** (1743–50) and Sidi Mohammed (1750–90) ruled over a weakened kingdom. **Sidi Mohammed** pursued peace with Christian nations, but his successors, in turn, tried to keep Morocco isolated from Europe with some short-lived success.

Above: *Sturdy stone arches once supported the roof of an ancient granary within the ramparts of Meknès, one of Morocco's four imperial cities.*

TOURISM EARNINGS

Tourism has become Morocco's second-largest earner of foreign currency and, in some places (such as Marrakech, Tangier and Agadir), directly or indirectly employs up to half the workforce. According to the **Morocco National Tourist Board**, visitor numbers are growing between 5 per cent and 9 per cent annually and exceed three million per year.

France and Spain

France began its determined conquest of North Africa in 1830 with the invasion of Algeria, which it completed in a series of campaigns that lasted until 1848. In 1832, the French navy bombarded Tangier and Eassaouira as punishment for Moroccan Sultan Moulay Abdul-Rahman's aid to the Algerian tribes, and in 1844 French troops pursued the Algerian rebel leader **Abdel Kader** across the border into Morocco.

Other powers were, however, also interested in the region. In 1856 the **Treaty of Tangier** opened the port to British trade, and in 1859 the Spanish seized Tetouan from their base at Ceuta. Growing numbers of European traders settled in Tangier and Casablanca, which were virtually ruled by European consuls. At the 1906 **Conference of Algeciras** the European powers agreed on a carve-up: Spain was to have Ceuta and parts of the north, as well as the southern Sahara region, while France would take the rest. The French began their occupation the following year in Casablanca, meeting resistance from the Saharan tribes with machine guns and repeating rifles, and by 1914 the European power controlled the central plains. World War I was to delay the conquest, but the French advance resumed in 1921. The last upsurge of resistance to European rule came from the Rif, where local chieftain **Abdel Krim** wiped out a Spanish army and drove the Spanish back to their coastal territories in 1921. Declaring a **Republic of the Rif**, Abdel Krim advanced into French-held Morocco in 1924 with an army of 120,000, but by 1926, caught between the modern armies of France and Spain, the Rif rising had been defeated. Sporadic guerrilla resistance nevertheless continued until 1936. The sultan remained the ruler of Morocco, but all real power was in the hands of the French resident-general (governor). The French proceeded to build roads and new administrative towns outside the walls of the old cities, and encouraged European investment in railways, mines and agriculture. Relatively few Europeans (around 300,000) actually settled in Morocco, and the economy was controlled by a small, wealthy elite, but it wasn't long before the majority of the Alaouite princes, provincial governors and merchants of Morocco's existing ruling class came to be hand in glove with the colonialists. Among the most powerful of these collaborationists were the **Berber** lords of the **High Atlas**, who had allied with the French against Abdel Krim in the 1920s.

During World War II, Morocco was governed by the **French Vichy government**, which cooperated with Nazi Germany to rule those areas of France not occupied by Axis forces.

This is the era in which the film *Casablanca* is set, when the French colonial capital became a hotbed of intrigue and espionage. In 1943, following American landings in Tunisia and the Allied defeat of Axis forces in North Africa, Morocco was 'liberated' by Free French forces.

> **POPULATION**
>
> Morocco's total population (1994 census) is just under 27 million, of whom 47 per cent are **under 20** and 51.4 per cent live in the **cities**. The population is almost evenly split between male and female, but men make up a much larger proportion (72 per cent) of the **working urban population**. The population is believed to be growing at around 2.2 per cent annually. Some 1,080,000 Moroccans live and work abroad, around half of this number in France.

Below: *The tanneries at Fez are among the city's most fascinating (and smelliest) points of interest, with skins curing in great pots of multicoloured dye.*

A MATTER OF
MATHEMATICS

Arab mathematicians of the early Middle Ages were vastly more sophisticated than their European counterparts as they had understood the **concept of zero** – a mathematical concept that was to elude the savants of Europe until several centuries later. The Arabaic word for zero, *sifr*, has entered the English language as **cipher**, meaning any complex mathematical puzzle.

Opposite: *Large posters of King Mohammed VI, who succeeded his father in 2000, are prominently displayed in towns and cities.*
Below: *Morocco's national flag displays a five-pointed star.*

Independence

After the end of World War II in 1945, France attempted to retain its colonial possessions in North Africa, but after a long and bloody war of independence, the colonists were eventually driven out of neighbouring Algeria. Resistance to French rule in Morocco was less violent, but in 1956 France nevertheless handed over power to **Sultan Mohammed V** (1956–61). Spain hung onto the Spanish Sahara (Western Sahara) until 1975 when it capitulated to Moroccan demands and international pressure and handed the territory over after **Hassan II** led a 300,000-strong Green March of Moroccans to occupy the territory. The **Saharawi people** of the south – who regard themselves as ethnically and culturally distinct – were, however, not all in favour of union with Morocco, and the **Polisario movement** has, from bases inside Algerian territory, fought Moroccan forces since the withdrawal of the Spanish. In an effort to counter Polisario's mobile guerrillas, the **Moroccan army** has, in the meanwhile, built a gigantic wall of sand to protect strategic targets in the south. The war is sparsely reported and travel to the south is restricted, but Polisario reportedly continues to mount hit-and-run attacks.

GOVERNMENT AND ECONOMY

Since his succession to the throne, Sultan Mohammed VI has reinforced tentative moves in the direction of multi-party democracy which began towards the end of his father's reign. In 1997, a bicameral legislature was introduced. This consists of the Chamber of Counsellors, with 270 members indirectly elected for a nine-year term by local councils, trades unions and professional organizations; and the 325-member Chamber of Representatives, elected by popular vote every five years. Thirty seats in the Chamber of

Representatives are reserved for women. The first multi-party elections were held in 2002, with the RNI (National Rally of Independents) emerging as the largest party in the Chamber of Counsellors with 42 seats, while the USFP (Socialist Union of Popular Forces) is the largest party in the Chamber of Representatives with 50 seats. Neither group has a governing majority, and in Morocco's

fledgling democracy the Chambers do little more than advise the monarch, who remains the country's unchallenged chief executive. The right to vote was extended to all Moroccans over 18 years of age in 2003. Elections to the Chamber of Counsellors were held in 2006, and elections to the Chamber of Representatives were held in 2007 but resulted in no significant changes.

Economic Development

Agriculture and **fisheries** comprise the most important sector of the economy, employing some 40 per cent of Moroccans and accounting for 30 per cent of the country's exports and 14 per cent of gross domestic product. A year-round growing season allows Morocco to export early- and late-season fruits and vegetables, and the country ships almost 199,000 tons of tomatoes and more than 50,000 tons of potatoes a year, mainly to Europe, North America and the Middle East. Beans, peppers, courgettes (zucchini), olives, cucumbers and fruit – including melons, strawberries, peaches and apricots – are also exported. With a coastline of about 3500km (2175 miles) and an offshore fishing zone extending 320km (200 miles) into the Atlantic, Morocco has an annual seafood haul of some 783,000 tons and exports US$680 million worth of marine products each year. The country has no oil, but is the world's largest source of **phosphates**, boasting some 75 per cent of the world's phosphate

SHIITES AND SUNNIS

The Prophet **Mohammed** was born in Mecca in 570AD and received his first revelation from God (Allah) at the age of 40. Soon he began preaching a new, monotheistic and ascetic religion, called **Islam**, meaning submission to the Will of God. The new faith grew quickly and, after his death in 632, spread across the Middle East under the leadership of his successors (caliphs). Mohammed had no sons, and in 661 his son-in-law Ali lost a struggle for the caliphate, which passed to a line of leaders who became known as the **Ommayads** or Ummayads and their followers, known as **Sunnis**. The heirs of Ali and his wife, Mohammed's daughter Fatima, became known as **Fatimids** and their followers as **Shiites**. Most of the Muslim world today (including Morocco) is Sunni, but the Shia sect flourishes in a number of Islamic countries.

Above: *Camel rides are a popular holiday experience for tourists like these at Zagora.*
Opposite: *Many Berber women still wear traditional chin tattoos and voluminous robes.*

resources. Exports of these minerals are a very important foreign-currency earner. In 2004 Morocco signed a free trade agreement with the USA, signalling new moves to open up its economy.

Under Hassan II, little effort was made to diversify or modernize the economy beyond these traditional sources of income, but one growth area has been the farming of **cut flowers** for export, with 90 million stems of roses exported each year. As a result of its authoritarian government and poor record in education and development, Morocco's economy stagnated during the 1980s and 1990s and harsh austerity measures were introduced at the behest of the International Monetary Fund. By the end of the 20th century, there were indications that the economy was improving, with **inflation** down to less than 3 per cent, but **per capita income** remains low in comparison with the developed world, at only US$1200 per year. Poor education and training nevertheless remain an obstacle to economic growth, with **literacy** levels lower than 70 per cent in cities and as low as 23 per cent in the countryside. In total, around 50 per cent of men and 70–80 per cent of Moroccan women cannot read.

Tourism

Few tourists (other than a handful of artists, scholars and adventurers) visited Morocco until the second half of the 20th century. In the 1950s, Morocco became a favoured hang-out of bohemian writers, artists, beatniks and a handful of wealthy socialites such as the Woolworths heiress, Barbara Hutton. Some were drawn by the readily available hashish, many simply by the country's fine beaches, warm weather and exotic culture. In the 1960s and 70s, young European and American travellers were also drawn by cheap and plentiful dope and the excitement of travel to a mysterious land only a few hours from western Europe. At the same time, package holidaymakers from France, Britain, Germany and Scandinavia were beginning to discover the delights of Morocco's beach destinations.

In 1960, the small southern Moroccan fishing port of **Agadir** was levelled by an earthquake (killing around 15,000 people) and King Hassan decided to reconstruct it as a purpose-built **tourism resort**. Attracting wealthy investors such as the French resort operator Club Med, Agadir is now the country's biggest and best-known package-holiday resort, attracting hundreds of thousands of visitors annually.

MOSQUE ARCHITECTURE

The mosque embodies the spirit of Islam and is typically a rectangular building with a large *haram* (prayer hall) divided into several aisles and with a number of entrances. In an adjoining courtyard stands a fountain, for Muslims must wash in running water before they pray. Midway along the *qibla*, or prayer wall, of the mosque is the *mihrab*, an arched niche showing the direction of Mecca, towards which the faithful must face when praying, and the *minbar*, or pulpit, from which the imam delivers the Friday *khutba* (sermon). On the opposite wall rises the minaret, a square tower from which the call to prayer is sounded.

THE PEOPLE

Over the millennia, many peoples and cultures have converged in Morocco – Romans, Carthaginians, Vandals and Visigoths, Sephardic Jews and Spanish and French colonialists.

Today, most of Morocco's approximately 34.75 million people (2007 estimate) are descendants of the **Arab** migrants who arrived in Morocco (bringing Islam with them) from the 7th century onwards, or of the **Berber** people who had already settled North Africa for many centuries before the arrival of the Arab. There has been much mingling of Arab and Berber over the centuries, though many communities – mainly in the Rif, Moyen Atlas and High Atlas – are of pure Berber stock. There is also a small **European** minority of around 60,000. Morocco had a substantial **Jewish** popula-

tion, which was swelled by Sephardic Jews expelled from intolerant Christian Spain after the Reconquista, but most Moroccan Jews emigrated to Israel during the 20th century, leaving a small and ageing population of around 30,000. The **Saharawi** (Saharan) people of the deep south (former Spanish Sahara, and today generally known as Western Sahara) also claim a separate ethnic identity.

Language

Arabic is the first language of all Moroccans, including the Berber and Saharawi minorities, though there are also three distinct **Berber dialects**: Rif, spoken in the Rif mountain communities; Tamazight, in the Moyen Atlas; and Chleuh, in the High Atlas. Although Arabic is one of the world's most widely spoken languages, with more than 800 million Arabic speakers from Morocco to the Arabian Sea, the Moroccan version is distinctive, with many dialect words and phrases and (to the Arab ear) a strong regional accent. **French** is Morocco's second language, and is spoken very widely and used on street and shop signs. Many Moroccans travel to France as migrant workers, and many wealthy families send their children to France to complete their education. King Mohammed V is one of this French-educated elite, with a doctorate from the University of Nice.

Religion

Virtually all Moroccans are **Muslims**, following the **Sunni** version of Islam. Religion is very much part of everyday life, with the call to prayers sung by a muezzin (or, more likely these days, broadcast from a tape player through loudspeakers) at sunrise, midday, afternoon, sunset and mid-evening. Most Moroccans prostrate themselves in prayer at these times wherever they happen to be. Many visit the mosque to pray daily

and almost all men attend midday prayers on Friday, when
the imam of each mosque reads
the weekly lesson, known as
the *khutba*, from the Koran.
Most also observe the fast of
Ramadan, the ninth month of
the Muslim calendar, when
nothing may pass their lips
between sunrise and sunset –
not even cigarette smoke.
Making the pilgrimage (*Haj*) to
Mecca, Islam's holiest city, is
considered a duty, though not
all Moroccans can afford to
perform it. In many villages, the
homes of those who have made
the *Haj* can be identified by
colourful, naive mural paintings
recording the journey.

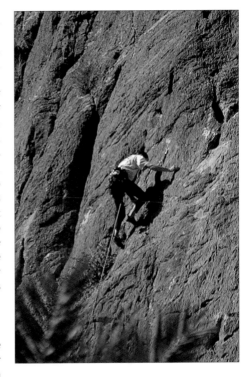

Sport and Recreation

Most Moroccans do not have
enough disposable income or
leisure time to take part in
sports that require much equipment or watch big-ticket
spectator events. **Football** is the most popular sport
among men, and Morocco regularly reaches the last
stages of major international championships, including
the 1994 and 1998 World Cup final rounds. Moroccan
players are widely head-hunted by top European clubs.
Competitive **cycling** (an enthusiasm caught from the
French) is also popular among those who can afford
a racing bike.

For the visitor with a taste for active sports, Morocco
is alluring, with a climate that allows for the playing of
most sports year round. Most luxury hotels have **tennis**
courts, and many are close to excellent 18-hole **golf**
courses. The mountains and foothills are perfect for
hiking and **cycling**, with the High Atlas offering some of

Above: *Rock climbing is
a newly popular pastime
on the steep, red cliffs
of the Todra Gorge.*
Opposite: *The minaret
mosque at Taroudannt,
with its patterned tiles
and crenellated tower,
is typical of traditional
Moroccan religious
architecture.*

Above: *Brightly coloured pots and dishes in both traditional and modern patterns for sale at a craft centre in Ouarzazate.*

the finest **mountain trekking** in the world. There is also excellent deep-sea **game fishing**. For riders, the range of terrain (and of mounts) is wide: choose from mule trekking in the Atlas, camel safaris in the desert, or horseback riding in all sorts of surroundings. Agadir is the best bet for **water sports**, which include surfing, waterski, windsurfing and dinghy sailing, and Essaouira is also highly rated by windsurfers. Scuba is also available, though there are no-world class dive sites.

Music

Traditional and classical Moroccan music, song and dance reflect the country's vital, multi-stranded heritage. **Berber** tradition is strongly musical, with small bands of balladeers wandering the countryside and performing songs that were often (and still are) a rich repository of tribal history, culture and oral folklore. Al-Andalus (Moorish Spain) has also left its mark, notably in the classical form known as *nawba*, and codified by the 9th-century Moorish master Ziryeb. In both traditions, string and percussion are the most important instruments, ranging from goatskin-covered Berber drums and tambourines to the lute-like *guimbri*, the *amzhad* (a simple violin) or the three-stringed *kanza*. Wind instruments include the *lira*, or reed flute, the trumpet-like *anda* and the *ghaita*, similar to the oboe.

As with the visual arts, the restrictions of Islam – which tends to frown on many forms of **dancing**, and especially on men and women dancing together – have limited the development of spectator and participatory dance in Morocco. In rural regions, traditional circle dances such as the *ahidous* and the *guedra* are reminiscent of those found throughout the southern Mediterranean region.

METALWORK

You will see smiths in every souk, working tin, brass, copper and silver to produce an array of household utensils and elaborate ornaments. Hammered and chased copper lamps, trays, jugs and plates can be good value, and even the humbler utensils can be attractive. Gold souks can be found in Fez and Meknès, and chunky Berber silver necklaces, bracelets and pendants can be found in southern towns such as Tiznit or Taroudannt. Beware of imitations – there is plenty of good work around, but there is an even larger supply of fake stuff made from thinly plated gold and silver, and even coloured plastic in place of valuable amber.

Art and Architecture

Of all the arts, architecture and design have flourished most strongly in Morocco. Strict Islam regards visual representation of any living thing as anathema: only Allah, the Creator, may create. In Morocco, this prohibition has given rise to a highly decorative but **abstract art**, using complex geometric patterns to adorn pottery, textiles, metalwork and ceramics. Much of the finest decorative stucco carving, *zellij* (mosaic) and calligraphy is found in mosques and medersas (Islamic schools), almost all of which are closed to non-Muslims, but some fine examples may be seen in those few mosques which do admit unbelievers. In such religious architecture, a common theme is the stylized arched gateway, meant as a reminder of the seven gates to Paradise. Such architectural details are also found in secular and domestic architecture. In many Berber settlements, the simple architecture of homes and other buildings – usually of mud brick – is very different from the elaborate style of Morocco's great mosques. Fortified buildings reflect a turbulent past: the ksour (castle-village), kasbah (miniature fortress of a village headman) and agadir (fortified grain store) are all reminders of a not too distant time when the best insurance policy was a well-constructed set of battlements.

Literature

Morocco has no great literary tradition of its own and, sadly, few works by its handful of better-known authors are accessible to English-speaking readers – largely because French is the preferred language for editions translated from the original Arabic.

Of those whose books are available in English translation, one of the best known is **Tahar ben Jelloun**, who lives in self-

---

THE *TAJINE*

Morocco's most characteristic **cooking vessel** is made of part-glazed terracotta, sometimes decorated with simple abstract or geometric patterns. The base is a deep circular dish in which all the aingredients are assembled. The conical lid makes an enclosed cooking space in which the aromas from the ingredients circulate. The *tajine* is designed for long, slow cooking on a low heat. Moroccan cooks say a hot fire destroys all the flavour of the dish. The best *tajines* are said to come from the village of **Oued Laou**, southeast of Tetouan on the Mediterranean coast, and are sold in souks all over Morocco. Tajines are cheap but fragile – if you plan to take one home, wrap and carry it very carefully.

Below: *Zagora is a good place to seek out vividly coloured Berber rugs and carpets like these.*

Above: *This famous road sign at Zagora harks back to the heyday of the camel caravans.*

imposed exile in France and has won that country's coveted literary award for *Solitaire*, a book about the problems of Moroccan emigrant workers in France. His novel *Silent Day in Tangier* has also been translated into English.

Morocco nevertheless appears as an exotic setting in the works of a wide range of English, American and European authors, including the American **Paul Bowles**, a long-time resident of Tangier.

Food and Drink

Moroccan cuisine is fragrant with **herbs** and **spices**: freshly roasted and ground cumin, rich golden saffron, and many more. A blend of ingredients called *ras al-hanut* is the key to Moroccan cooking, and most dishes contain one or more of these subtle flavourings, as well as garlic, ginger, or coriander. Unique to Moroccan cooking is the use with meat or poultry of flavourings Westerners most commonly associate with sweet desserts, such as honey, cinnamon, almonds and powdered sugar. Traditionally, much cooking was done overnight in the communal village bread oven, using the *tajine*, a heavy terracotta dish with a distinctive conical lid that has lent its name to what is really Morocco's national dish, a succulent **stew** of meat or fish and vegetables cooked in their own juices for up to 12 hours and eaten as the main meal of the day. These hearty dishes are especially popular in Morocco's mountain communities in winter, when **root vegetables** such as sweet potato and carrot come into the markets and are combined with spiced veal, mutton and chicken. *Tajine* is usually served with **couscous**, the starchy cereal that is to Moroccan cooking what pasta is to Italian, or rice to

CUMIN

Cumin has been used around the Mediterranean for around 4000 years and, although it plays hardly any part in European cooking, it is still one of the most important flavours in North African dishes. Moroccans are especially fond of the roast and freshly ground seeds as an embellishment to simple fish dishes. The spice is usually added at the end of cooking or sprinkled onto the finished dish for maximum flavour.

Chinese dishes. Another legendary Moroccan dish is *bastilla*, a rich and complex **pigeon pie** made with the paper thin pastry known as *warqa* (also used in a range of sweet and savoury dishes). Originating in Fez, *bastilla* is on the menu at the best restaurants nationwide and is not to be missed. In fishing ports such as Ksar es Seghir and Essaouira, fresh **seafood** features prominently on the menu. Sample delicious sardines freshly caught and cooked at simple stalls right on the harbour, or try more expensive fish dishes such as stuffed sea bass in more sophisticated eating places. *Samneh* (clarified butter) is traditionally used in dishes that require frying, but many people now prefer to use lighter oils such as sunflower or corn oil.

Despite opposition from strict Muslims, Morocco continues to make **wine** from domestically grown grapes, and also imports it from Europe. Most Moroccan wines are unsophisticated reds with a high alcohol content, and light, pilsner-style **beer** is also widely available.

Alcohol, however, is rarely available within the walls of the old towns, where people tend to be more traditional in outlook, and is usually served only in the bars and restaurants of tourist hotels.

During the Muslim fasting month of Ramadan, alcohol may not be served at all or may only be served to non-Muslims in private. The drink of choice for most Moroccans is **mint tea**, served sweet and piping hot in small glasses and drunk at any time of day or night. The offer of a glass of tea is the most basic form of hospitality, and it is rude to refuse. Shopkeepers will often offer you a glass of tea while you haggle over prices.

> **MINT TEA**
>
> Although Moroccans some-times drink black or red tea, mint tea is always made with finely ground green, or 'gunpowder', tea. Sugar – traditionally chipped from a large block – is added to the pot, and fresh leaves of green mint (*mentha viridis*) are infused in the tea to give it its unique flavour.

Below: *An orange-seller at a market in Agadir.*

2. Tangier and the Mediterranean Coast

Morocco's Mediterranean coast extends some 510km (320 miles) from Tangier in the west to Saïdia in the east, with the Mediterranean narrowing to the Strait of Gibraltar where it meets the Atlantic Ocean at Cap Spartel, the northwest tip of the African continent. Along this coast is a chain of black and white sand **beaches**, while only a few kilometres inland rise the slopes of the **Rif mountains**.

For centuries, this region of Morocco has been more influenced by Europe than any other part of the country, and this is evident in the **Spanish-Moroccan** architecture of towns such as Tangier and Tetouan, the **Portuguese** fortifications of Ksar es Seghir, a scattering of **French** and **Hispanic** place names and, of course, in the enclaves of Ceuta and Melilla, which are still ruled by **Spain**.

Hot and sunny in summer, cool and wet in winter (due to the influence of the Atlantic as well as the Rif mountains), northern Morocco has a **mellow climate**, spectacular scenery and fascinating historic towns to explore. It is no surprise to find that it has been discovered by **tourism**; what is more surprising is that it has not yet been much developed, with only a handful of holiday resorts dotted along the Mediterranean coast. A visit to this region of mountains, beaches and Berber villages can be the perfect introduction to Morocco.

TANGIER

Tangier still has more than a whiff of the **cosmopolitan** atmosphere for which it was once famous. A meeting

DON'T MISS

*** Grand Socco: old market area with craft shops.
*** Chefchaouen: the most dazzling town in the Rif mountains.
** Dar el-Makhzen (Royal Palace) **and Ethnographical and Archaeological Museum:** interesting collection of historic relics.
* Cap Spartel, **Grottes d'Hercule** and **Cotta:** great view and remains of ancient Roman town.
* Museum of Contemporary Art: the country's best collection of modern Moroccan art.

Opposite: With its Arabic and Spanish architecture, Tangier is a city of contrasts.

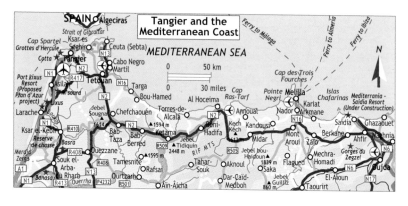

place of Mediterranean cultures for more than 2000 years, the city was always Europe's **gateway to Morocco**, a role that was reinforced in 1923 when it was placed under the government of an international authority, with representatives from Belgium, Britain, France, Italy, the Netherlands, Portugal, Sweden, Spain and the USA. The authority's main purpose was to satisfy each of these interested powers that Tangier's **strategic harbour** remained neutral. There was little interest in policing the city or regulating its trade, and Tangier became notorious as a city where anything could be enjoyed – for a price.

Parts of the city are still somewhat seedy, and visitors arriving on the ferry from Spain will be confronted by a mass of hustlers touting for hotels or offering their services as guides. Prostitution and drug abuse have much lower profiles than in the past but are still evident.

That said, Tangier remains a very popular spot to begin a Moroccan journey, with a lively atmosphere, a labyrinthine medina (market area), a pleasant climate, good beaches and some interesting architecture that reflects its variegated history.

The Grand Socco ★★★

The heart of the city is the Grand Socco, officially called the Place 9 Avril 1947. *Socco* is a Hispanic version of the Moroccan souk (market) and this square truly is the city's

---

FALSE GUIDES

Generally known as *faux-guides* (false guides), the young men who hang around almost every cheap hotel and bus and rail station in Morocco are the country's greatest pests. Particularly numerous and persistent in **Tangier** and **Tetouan**, they will offer to guide you through the medina, show you the sights or find you a hotel, ostensibly out of friendship, then attempt to pester or bully you into paying an exorbitant fee. The government has attempted to make their activities illegal, with perhaps unduly harsh prison sentences, but 'guiding' is a tempting career choice for unemployed youths in a society where poverty endures.

main marketplace, especially on Thursday and Sunday each week, with the arrival of a veritable caravan of farming folk from the Rif – wearing their trademark wide-brimmed straw hats or red-and-white striped poncho-like garments called *foutas* – who lay out heaps of fresh **fruit** and **vegetables** for sale. When not in use as a produce market, the square is crammed with traffic, from motor-cycles and pickup trucks to handcarts and the occasional donkey. It is also the gateway to Tangier's medina, reached via the Rue Semmarine and the Rue des Siaghines (Rue as-Siaghin), lined with tacky souvenir shops.

Jardins de la Mendoubia ★

On the west side of the Grand Socco a prominent door opens into the Mendoubia Gardens, where the highlight is a gnarled, ancient **fig tree**, said to be some 800 years old and to imprison the spirit of a wicked prince who ruled the city in the 13th century. Open 08:00–21:00 daily.

Sidi Bou Abid Mosque ★

Built in 1917, the **minaret** of this colourful mosque, decorated in geometric patterns of red, green, blue and yellow tiles, dominates the Grand Socco. Though open to Muslims daily (24 hours), it is not open to non-Muslims.

The Medina ★★

After negotiating the tourist tat of the Rue as-Siaghin, you will find yourself on the **Petit Socco**, once one of the hubs of Tangier's low-life but now just a small square with a handful of open-air cafés and busy with passers-by. The medina is one of the oldest parts of the city and is a maze of narrow streets, often festooned overhead with drying laundry and dangerous-looking tele-

> **HENRI MATISSE**
>
> A visit to Tangier in 1912 marked a turning point for the French painter Henri Matisse (1869–1954), who produced more than 60 drawings and paintings during his stay in Morocco and was inspired by the colours of the medina and by the patterns of Moroccan *zellij* work, carving and weaving to create his unique and highly stylized blend of **abstract** and **representational art**.

Below: *Though Tangier is a tourist town, its streets are lined with traditional shops and thronged with people in traditional dress.*

KASBAH, MEDINA AND SOUK

Sometimes used loosely in modern English, these terms have precise meanings. The **medina** of any Moroccan town is the old town centre, usually walled and with a maze of narrow streets and lanes, most – or all – of them impassable to vehicles. Some medinas are almost 1000 years old and among the oldest continuously inhabited settlements in the world. Within each medina are **souks**. Each souk may be just a section of street or several streets together, and each specializes in a particular trade or product, such as leatherwork, silversmithing or rug weaving. The **kasbah** is the most strongly fortified section of the medina, usually built as the castle of a sultan of local chieftain. In the Atlas and the south, 'kasbah' also refers to fortified villages.

phone and electricity cables. The medina is **densely populated**, and many of its merchants and craftspeople have their homes on the upper floors of buildings that house their shops and workshops. Walking through its streets, be prepared to put up a determined resistance to shopkeepers who urge you to 'just look' at their wares – once inside, it's not easy to leave their shops without being pressured into buying something.

American Legation Museum ★

Enter the medina through the southern gate, off Rue du Portugal, onto a narrow and nameless lane and turn left to find this three-storey building, given to the USA by **Sultan Moulay Suleyman** in 1820. Now a small museum financed by the US Information Service, it has a library of **historical documents** of interest mainly to scholars. The museum is open Wednesday–Monday 09:00–18:00.

The Kasbah ★★★

In the northwest corner of the medina is the kasbah, a **walled enclave** that was once the home of sultans. Many of its most stylish and luxurious houses are now owned by wealthy expatriates.

Four gates lead from the outer medina through the walls of the kasbah. It is easiest to enter through the **Bab el-Assa**, which leads directly to the kasbah's main attraction, the former Royal Palace.

Museum of Moroccan Art ★★

Housed in the 17th-century Royal Palace (Dar el-Makhzen) of Sultan Moulay Ismail, this museum features archaic firearms and swords, mosaic tile work,

Tangier

and ancient Arabic manuscripts. Next to it, the **Museum of Antiquities** displays finds from Morocco's Roman-era archeological sites, Lixus, Cotta and Volubilis, including bronzes and mosaics, along with relics of the even earlier Carthaginian presence on the country's Mediterranean coast. Dar el-Makhzen, Place de la Kasbah, open Wednesday–Monday 09:00–18:00.

Above: *Palm trees and tall old mansions dominate Tangier's skyline.*

Sultan's Gardens ★
Surrounding the former palace, the gardens are shaded by **palms** and fragrant with **orange** and **lemon** blossom. Open 09:00–15:30 (April–October), 09:00–12:30 and 15:00–17:30 (November–March), daily except Tuesday.

VILLE NOUVELLE
The dull new town (built in the 1930s to house the head-quarters of the foreign representatives and international commerce) is in sharp contrast to the hustle and bustle of the old medina – but you may feel that this is no bad thing, as fending off the advances of the medina's more aggressive salesmen can be exhausting. The **cafés** dotted around the Place de France and the Terrasse des Paresseux are a pleasant place to relax with an evening drink, and there are **great views** across the Strait of Gibraltar – only 14km (9 miles) wide at this point – from the Terrasse des Paresseux.

GOLDEN APPLES

Hercules, the mythical hero noted for his strength and courage, has been associated with Morocco since ancient times, when according to legend he was sent here to steal from the **Garden of Hesperides** the legendary golden apples, now thought to be the fruit Europeans came to know as **tangerines** (after Tangier, the port from which they were first exported to Europe).

Museum of Contemporary Art ★

Formerly the British Consulate, this building at 52 Rue d'Angleterre is now the main showcase for modern Moroccan artists. In a country without a strong tradition of representational art, the paintings of artists such as **Moulay Ahmed Idrissi** and **Abdallah Hariri** stand out. It is open 08:30–12:00 and 14:00–18:30, Wednesday–Monday.

CAP SPARTEL

Some 14km to the west of Tangier, the northwestern tip of Africa is marked by a lighthouse at Cap Spartel. To the ancient Greeks, it was also the westernmost limit of the known world, where the Mediterranean opened into the Atlantic Ocean, which they believed to be infinitely large. In spring and autumn, **birders** know it as an excellent location to spot many of the migrant species flying between Africa and Europe. It is worth a visit if only for the **scenic coastal drive** from Tangier.

Grottes d'Hercule ★

About 4km (2½ miles) south of the Cap Spartel, the **Caves of Hercules** are natural grottos carved by the sea from limestone cliffs. Legend says Hercules rested in these caverns after completing his labours, and that he created the headlands known to the ancient Greeks and Romans as the 'Pillars of Hercules' – known as **Gibraltar** (Jebel Tariq) in Europe and **Jebel Musa** in Morocco – by pushing the mountains apart to create the Strait of Gibraltar. The grottos are open from 09:00 to sunset daily.

Cotta ★

Just 500m (1650ft) inland from the caves lie the tumbled columns and walls of Cotta, a small **Roman settlement** dating from the 2nd and 3rd centuries BC, where archaeologists have unearthed parts of the walls and public buildings, including a **bathhouse**, **villa** and **temple**. Most interesting are the remnants of

---

THE PILLARS OF HERCULES

The cartographers of the ancient Hellenic world, whose colonies in the western Mediterranean included Sicily and Marseilles, knew the **Straits of Gibraltar**, the narrows between Gibraltar and Tangier, as the Pillars of Hercules and regarded them as the limit of the known world. Beyond, they thought, lay nothing but the empty ocean and the land of **Ultima Thule**, the islands at the ends of the earth. More pragmatic Phoenician seafarers sailed as far as southwest England – where they traded for tin – and south along the Moroccan coast as far as their colony of Mogador and beyond.

large mortar-lined **storage vats** used for oil and garum, the fish sauce that was the most popular seasoning in Roman cooking (similar to the nam pla fish extract used in Vietnamese, Thai and Chinese cooking today) and was probably Cotta's main export. Open from 09:00 to sunset daily.

ASILAH

Asilah, about 46km (29 miles) south of Tangier on the Atlantic coast, has had a turbulent past. Founded by the Carthaginians and conquered by the Romans, it was seized by the Portuguese in 1471, retaken by the Moroccans in 1589, captured by Spain, and retaken by Sultan Moulay Ismail in 1691. In the late 19th and early 20th century, it was the lair of the notorious bandit pasha, **Mohammed er-Raissouli**. The 15th-century **Portuguese fortifications** are a legacy of this troubled history, but today Asilah is a dinky, post-card-pretty place with a new yacht harbour, plenty of attractively restored homes, a good beach and lots of local colour.

The Medina **

Enclosed by Portuguese battlements, Asilah's old medina is less commercial and more picturesque than that of Tangier. In August each year, Asilah hosts a **festival of the arts**, when the town becomes one big gallery with paintings exhibited in the Raissouli Palace, in the streets and even painted on the walls of houses – you'll see a number of these as you walk through the medina.

The walls on the sea-ward side of the medina are the most accessible, giving a **good view** of the city and its surroundings.

> ### TARIQ'S MOUNTAIN
>
> The first Muslim invasion of Europe was led by a Berber general, **Tariq Ibn Ziyad**, whose 7000-strong army defeated the last Visigoth king of Spain, Roderic, outside **Jerez de la Frontera** in 711. His first beachhead was on the rocky peninsula that still bears his name – Gibraltar, a corruption of 'Jebel Tariq' which means 'Tariq's Mountain'.

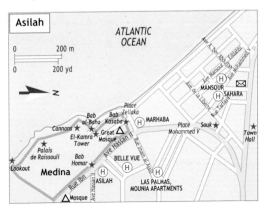

TANGIER BEACHES

Don't visit Tangier for its beaches, which are no more than adequate, polluted in places and frequented by hustlers, dope dealers, pickpockets and (after dark) muggers. For better beaches, head east of the city to the finer beaches around **Asilah**, **Ksar es Seghir** or the resorts south of **Ceuta**.

Palais de Raissouli ★★

Built for the rogue pasha Er-Raissouli in 1909, this **bijou palace** is located about midway along the sea wall of the medina. It houses a changing programme of **exhibitions** and **events**. The palace is open 08:30–12:30 and 15:00–18:00, Saturday–Thursday.

M'soura ★

Approximately 25km (16 miles) southeast of Asilah and 6km (4 miles) north of Tnine Sidi el-Yamani village, the enigmatic circle of **stone monoliths** (the tallest of which is about 6m/20ft high) may mark the grave of a Carthaginian nobleman.

LARACHE

Like Asilah and Ksar es Seghira, Larache was once a Portuguese and Spanish stronghold, but its walls have been dismantled and only a small **fortified kasbah** and miniature **Spanish castle** remain. Bigger and rather less pretty than Asilah, it also sees fewer visitors but there are **beaches** nearby.

Below: *The harbour at Asilah is lined with buildings reminiscent of the Spanish colonial era.*

Kasbah de la Cigogne **

The Kasbah de la Cigogne (Stork Castle) is named for the **storks** that sometimes nest on its decrepit towers. Built by the Spanish in the 17th century, it is currently closed to visitors.

Archaeological Museum *

Housed in another former Spanish stronghold, the museum contains a not very impressive collection of finds from **Lixus**, the Roman archaeological site nearby. It is open 09:00–12:00 and 15:00–18:00, Wednesday–Monday.

Above: *Strong Atlantic winds make the Moroccan coast ideal for windsurfing.*

Lixus **

The interesting remains of the Roman city of Lixus lie approximately 5km (3 miles) north of Larache. Founded by Phoenicians as early as 1000BC, the city flourished as a Roman outpost from the first to the third century AD. Abandoned with the collapse of the western Roman empire in the 5th century AD, its most striking sights include the restored **amphitheatre** and **baths**, but much of the site is very dilapidated and overgrown.

There are fine views over the **Loukos River**, and the wetlands around the river offer great **birding**, with plenty of waterbirds, including spoonbill and ibis. The site is not fenced in, so you can visit it at any time.

THE MEDITERRANEAN COAST

Beaches of white and black sand – some crowded, some relatively undiscovered – as well as pebbly coves and sandy creeks are typical of the Mediterranean coast, where you can choose to stay in purpose-built resort hotels or in simple fishing villages.

CAP MALABATA

Cap Malabata, 10km (6 miles) east of Tangier, is the eastern 'horn' of the bay on which the city stands and is

---

PLAN D'AZUR

In 2006 the Moroccan government unveiled the Plan d'Azur, an ambitious project that is already changing the face of the country's Mediterranean and Atlantic coastline. Developers are being encouraged, through tax breaks and other incentives, to build vast residential and leisure complexes, golf courses and marinas on similar lines to Spain's Costa del Sol. The first of these are expected to open on the Mediterranean coast in 2008.

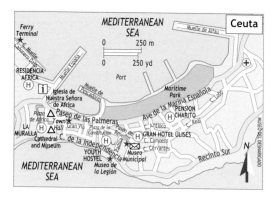

Opposite: Fishing boats in the harbour of the shabby seaside town and fishing port of Al Hoceima.

crowned by a prominent **lighthouse**, offering excellent views of the city and the bay. The Moroccan government has grandiose plans to develop this area as a complex of resort hotels, conference facilities, marinas and casinos.

Ksar es Seghir ★★

Only 37km (23 miles) to the east of Tangier and linked to the city by bus, Ksar es Seghir is an attractive **fishing town**, built within and around battlements constructed by the Portuguese in the 16th century. It is much calmer and less intimidating than the city, and you could quite easily base yourself here and visit the sights of Tangier on a day trip. Ksar es Seghir sees relatively few European tourists, but its **beaches** and good **seafood restaurants** make it a popular spot with Tangier residents in summer.

Ceuta (Sebta)

The Spanish enclave of Ceuta (called Sebta by the Moroccans) is 64km (40 miles) east of Tangier, and stands at the end of a promontory in the Mediterranean, within sight of the Spanish mainland port of Algeciras. With a mixed Spanish, Berber and Arab population of 75,000, Ceuta feels far more Spanish than Moroccan. Other than as a point of entry by **ferry from Spain**, it is of little interest to the visitor. If you have time to kill while waiting for transport, there are three small **museums**, all of which owe more to Spain than to Morocco.

Museo de la Legión ★

Like the French Foreign Legion, the Spanish Legion was created (in the 1920s) to do Spain's colonial dirty work. On Paseo de Colon, this is its museum, with a clutter of battle honours, medals, and mementoes of the fascist **General Francisco Franco**, whom the Legion helped to make dictator of Spain. Open Monday–Saturday 10:00–13:30, Sunday 16:00–18:00.

Housed in the 19th-century Castillo del Desnarigado, a fortress built at the southern end of the peninsula on which Ceuta stands, **Museo del Desnarigado** is another military museum with a small collection of uniforms and weapons. Open 11:00–14:00 and 16:00–18:00, weekends and public holidays.

Museo Municipal ★
On Calle Ingenieros (at the corner of Paseo del Revellin), this museum features a ramshackle **local history** collection. Open Jun–Sep Tue–Sat 10:00–14:00 and 19:00–21:00, Sun 11:00–14:00; Oct–May Tue–Sat 10:00–14:00 and 17:00–20:00, Sun 10:00–14:00.

THE RESORT COAST
South of the Spanish enclave at Sebta (Ceuta), the coast boasts several attractive, purpose-built beach resorts, with three- and four-star hotels, beaches, yacht harbours, water sports and land-based activities such as golf and tennis. This part of the Mediterranean has a Moroccan flavour, but the restaurants here have more in common with similar spots in Spain, Portugal, France and Italy than with their mountainous hinterland. Blue water, golden sand and lush green countryside make this an attractive area for a **beach holiday** in spring, summer or autumn. **Restinga Smir**, the northernmost of these coastal resorts, has an attractive new marina lined with glistening yachts and motor cruisers. **M'diq** and **Martil** have some good hotels and restaurants, while **Cabo Negro** has one of the country's best golf courses, the nine-hole Cabo Negro Royal Golf Club.

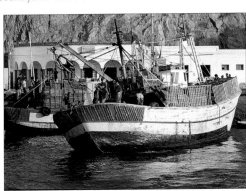

AL HOCEIMA

The shabby seaside town of Al Hoceima is partly redeemed by two small **beaches**, and is not a bad spot to pause for the night if you are exploring northern Morocco as an independent traveller, as it has plentiful accommodation and a pleasant location. Once a Spanish garrison town, it was founded as recently as 1920 and has no fascinating history or sights worth seeing.

MELILLA

Below: *In spring, melting snows and spring rains turn the slopes of the Rif mountains into colourful wildflower meadows.*

Like Ceuta, Melilla is Spanish territory and has been for centuries. If anything, it feels even more Spanish than Ceuta, with grim medieval walls and turrets surrounding the peninsula that shelters its **natural harbour**, now mainly used by Spanish trawlers. The **old town** (Melilla la Vieja, also called Medina Sidonia) inside these walls is worth a look if you have time to kill, but there are no museums or major attractions.

SAIDIA

Saidia, close to the Algerian border and 80km (50 miles) east of Melilla, is really the end of the Mediterranean road. There is no border crossing, so for most people there is little point in coming here except in August, when it is crowded with Moroccan visitors to the **annual festival of folk music**. It has an adequate **beach**, which – like the town – is usually uncrowded.

Gorges du Zegzel ★

For devotees of striking **geology**, some 28km (17 miles) to the south of Saidia the road S403 passes through the dramatic limestone Zegzel Gorges, stained with mineral deposits, on the way to Oujda and the main N17 highway south.

Oujda is a large but rather dull border town (the border crossing is closed) of no interest to the visitor except as a way station for those heading south.

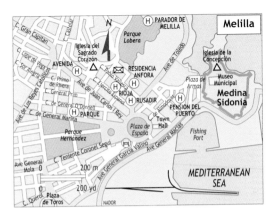

Grotte du Chameau ★

At the north end of the Zegzel Gorges, the so-called 'Cave of the Camel' is the largest of several limestone grottos in the region, and takes its name from a **stalagmite** that is said to resemble a camel. At the time of writing, it is not enclosed and can be visited at any time with a good torch; however, one of the local people may insist on 'guiding' you for a fee.

THE RIF MOUNTAINS

The fertile, cedar-clad slopes of the Rif mountains stretch in a crescent, roughly parallel to the Mediterranean coast, and rise to peaks of 1800–2000m (5900–6500ft), meeting the Moyen Atlas at their eastern end to form a near-impregnable **natural fortress** that allowed their inhabitants to remain proudly independent for much of history, and to resist conquest by European powers as late as the 1920s. Traditional **Berber mountain culture** still flourishes here.

Though no longer completely beyond the reach of the law, the Rif is still difficult terrain to police, and the **cannabis** trade continues to flourish here, centring on the raffish Rif town of Ketama (best avoided), where hashish is processed and exported in quantity to Europe. This is a face of Morocco very different from the rampant commercialism of Tangier or the burgeoning tourism along the Mediterranean coast. With few exceptions, life moves at

SOAP OR DOPE?

Low-grade Moroccan **hashish** – called 'soapbar' because of its shape – may contain only small amounts of *tetra hydrocannabinol* (THC), the active ingredient in cannabis, and a witch's brew of other substances including henna, shoe polish, coffee, diesel oil and liquorice, as well as the major tranquillizer *Largactil* to add a physical kick. Good reasons to steer well clear of any deals you may be offered.

Above: *Each Berber clan has its own characteristic style of carpet weaving, and patterns could even be used to convey messages.*

Opposite: *Colourful plates make attractive souvenirs.*

a slower pace here and there is time to experience the atmosphere of smaller towns and village markets at a gentler pace than in the city. Markets and artisans' workshops in the medinas of **Tetouan**, **Chefchaouen** and other Rif communities can be great places to pick up good-quality examples of Moroccan **rug weaving**, **metalwork** and **wood carving**. The Rif also has excellent **hiking** through forested hills and valleys, and Chefchaouen is the recommended base from which to **trek** the mountains.

TETOUAN

Some 68km (42 miles) southeast of Tangier, Tetouan looks down from its lofty position on the eastern slopes of the Rif mountains in the valley of the **Martil River** over the resorts of the coast to the Mediterranean. The main town of the northern Rif, Tetouan was the capital of Spanish Morocco from 1913 to 1956, and its characteristic **architecture** is very much influenced by **Spain**.

Typical of the city are the **ceramic tiles** that decorate many buildings and the **wrought-iron balconies** that sprout from upper windows. Spanish influence was not always benign; in 1399, the city was sacked by King Enrique III of Castile and lay in ruins until it was rebuilt by refugees from Granada after the Christian reconquest of Al-Andalus. Most of the city is relatively modern, and Spanish is still more widely spoken here (as a second language) than French.

Tetouan has long been notorious for the rapacious greed of the hustlers and touts who mob most visitors, offering to find them a hotel and guide them through its medina. These guys do themselves and their compatriots no favours, as the town's reputation causes many people to spend as little time here as possible, but those

LEATHERWARE

Moroccan leatherwear has a high reputation, and a wide range of footwear, coats and jackets, bags, wallets and accessories – both traditional and Western styles – can be found in the souks and in shops in the new town areas. Most of this is made for export, but more authentic ware includes the colourful soft slippers, called *babouches*, which almost all Moroccans still wear. They are colour-coded by gender – unornamented yellow or white for men, and red, pink and other colours and embroidered patterns for women.

who stay will discover a smattering of interesting sights, including a few small but interesting **museums** and **craft workshops**. Tetouan has a reputation as a centre of artisanship, with craftsmen specializing in leatherwork, carpentry, carving and especially embroidery. These crafts were Tetouan's main source of income until the 1980s, when tourism and other more modern industries finally caught up with the town. It is also a good place to shop for **traditional Berber textiles**, especially in the **Souk el-Hots**, the section of the medina specializing in Berber rugs and *foutas*.

Place Hassan II is the central square of the city, with the Bab er-Rouah on its southeast corner leading into the medina, and Calle Mohammed V running from the west side of the square through the middle of the new town.

Musée des Arts et Traditions Populaires ★★

Just south of Bab el-Okla, the gate that leads into the medina from the east, off Avenue Hassan II, the most interesting exhibits in the small Museum of Popular Art include **jewellery**, **embroidery** and **metalwork** dating back to Tetouan's 16th-century renaissance. Open 08:30–12:00 and 14:30–18:30, Monday–Friday.

School of Traditional Arts and Crafts ★★

Established more than half a century ago, the school overlooks beautiful **gardens** and aims to preserve the traditional skills for which Tetouan is famous. Here, children aged 10–18 years learn weaving, carpentry, leatherwork, mosaic and other skills from master craftsmen. A visit to this centre opposite Bab el-Okla is an excellent way to appreciate the amount of work that goes into making the goods you see

in the medina, but in a **less commercial** environment. The school is open 08:30–12:00 and 14:30–18:30, Monday–Friday (closed during school holidays).

Ensemble Artisanal ★★

This Craftsmens' Cooperative is a government-sponsored emporium (just across Avenue Hassan II from the park outside the southern wall of the medina) and is one of the best places in Morocco to buy well-made **Moroccan craftwork**, free of the aggressive haggling of medina salesmen. Prices here are more-or-less fixed, though you may negotiate a discount for cash. Open 09:00–12:30 and 15:30–18:30, Monday–Friday.

Musée Archeologique ★

The best thing about this small archaeology museum is its quiet **garden**, filled with Muslim and Jewish **tombstones** from 16th- and 17th-century Tetouan. Inside there is a small collection of coins and mosaics excavated at **Lixus** (see page 45). The museum is open 08:30–12:00 and 14:30–18:30, Monday–Friday.

CHEFCHAOUEN

Sometimes simply called Chaouen, Chefchaouen – 59km (37 miles) south of Tetouan – is the prettiest and most welcoming town in the Rif, with less of the money-grubbing mentality of Tetouan. Overlooked by the double-peaked **Jebel Chaouen** (the 'horned mountain'), it stands almost 1000m (3300ft) above sea level and in summer it is noticeably cooler than the coast. The minarets of more than 20 **mosques** rise high above the tiled roofs of its characteristic white-and-blue painted, two-storey houses.

Like Tetouan, Chefchaouen was settled in the early 16th century by Muslims and Jews fleeing Spanish persecution after the reconquest of Spain. Spanish troops occupied Chefchaouen in 1920, were driven out by the great Rif rebel chief **Abd el-Krim** in 1924, and reoccupied the town from 1926 until Morocco

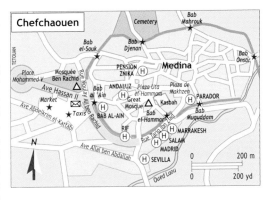

Chefchaouen map, showing: Bab Mahrouk, Cemetery, Bab el-Souk, Bab Djenan, Bab Onsar, PENSION ZNIKA, Medina, Place Mohammed V, Mosquée Ben Rachid, Ave Hassan II, ANDALUZ, Plaza Uta el-Hammam, Plaza de Makhzen, PARADOR, Market, Bab al 'Ain, Great Mosque, Kasbah, Taxis, Ave Abdelkrim el-Kattabi, BAB AL-AIN, Bab el-Hammam, Bab Muquddam, RIF, MARRAKESH, Ave Allal ben Abdallah, SALAM, MADRID, SEVILLA, Oued Loou, 0 200 m, 0 200 yd

gained independence in 1956 – but the Spanish influence is, in fact, less noticeable here than it is in Tetouan.

The Medina ★★★

Chefchaouen's medina is a delight, as it is small and easy to find your way around, and quite hassle free. **Weaving**, mainly of sheeps' and goats' wool, is one of the main occupations. Bab al 'Ain (Gate of the Spring) connects the relatively small new town with the medina, the hub of which is Plaza Uta el-Hammam, ringed by **cafés** and overlooked by a dilapidated 17th-century **kasbah** and the **Great Mosque**, dating from the 15th century (the mosque is not open to non-Muslims). A second, smaller square, the Plaza de Makhzen, is shaded by trees and surrounded by **souvenir shops**.

The Kasbah ★

The battered red-brick kasbah was built during the reign of **Moulay Ismail**. In the 1920s, Abd el-Krim made the fortress his own, but was humiliatingly imprisoned in his own dungeons after defeat by Spain in 1926. You can still see the cells in which he is said to have been held, just inside the entrance. Opposite is a small **museum** with a shabby collection of swords, daggers, muskets, and musical instruments, but it is worth visiting for the excellent **view of the medina** from the roof. It is open 09:00–13:00 and 15:00–18:30 daily.

Opposite: *Market day in Chefchaouen, today the most welcoming and picturesque of the Rif mountain towns.*

MEDINA DWELLERS

The blank walls facing onto the streets of a typical medina give little clue to what may lie within. Medina buildings rarely have any windows facing outward. Instead, their rooms look inward onto an inner **courtyard** or **garden**. Within may be overcrowded apartments housing numerous families, or the gracious home of one wealthy household. The twin hubs of the medina are its **mosque** – a social rendezvous as well as the heart of religious life – and the **hammam** (public bath house), like the mosque a vital meeting place, especially for women.

Tangier and the Mediterranean Coast at a Glance

Tangier can be visited year-round but is sunniest from Jun to Sep and can be cool and wet from Jan to Mar. The best times are from Apr to Jun and from Sep to Oct.

By Air: British Airways (www.ba.com) flies to Tangier from London several times weekly.
By Sea: Ferries to/from Spain, Italy and France: Comanav, tel: (039) 94 23 59, www.comanov.co.ma sails to Tangier from Algeciras and Almeria in Spain, from Sete and Port-Vendres in France, and from Genoa in Italy.
By Rail: Trains go from Tangier to Rabat (6 hours), Casablanca (7 hours), Marrakech (13 hours), Fez (5 hours) and Meknès (4 hours). Railway station, Place de la Marche Verte, Tangier, tel: (039) 93 45 70.
By Road: CTM buses operate frequently to Casablanca and Tetouan from Tangier to Casablanca, Rabat, Meknès, Fez and Marrakech. Local buses also connect Tangier with Larache and Asilah on the Atlantic coast, Tetouan, Chefchaouen and other points in the Rif, and all the towns along the Mediterranean coast. Long-distance taxis also run between all points in this section.

Use **taxis** in Tangier and elsewhere. Fares are cheap but must be firmly agreed in advance. **Buses** are not recommended. Bus and taxi station, Sahat Al Jamia al Arabia, Tangier, tel: (039) 94 66 82. **Horse-drawn carriages** are a picturesque (and pleasantly cool) way to travel, but quite expensive.

Tangier
LUXURY
Hôtel el-Minzah, 85 Rue de la Liberté, tel: (039) 94 23 59, www.elminzah.com Lavish five-star hotel with character, housed in a historic building.
Hôtel Club Le Mirage, Grottes d'Hercule, Cap Spartel, tel: (039) 33 33 32, www.lemirage-tanger.com Luxurious resort hotel, out-of-town location.

MID-RANGE
Ramada Almohades, Av des FAR, tel: (039) 94 07 55, www.ramada.com Excellent value for money, a handy location and the best of the hotels along the Tangier sea front.

BUDGET
Hôtel Continental, Rue dar el-Baroud (midway between Dar el-Baroud and Bab el-Marsa gates, just inside the medina walls), tel: (039) 93 10 24, www.s-h-systems.co.uk/morocco This once grand hotel is atmospheric and affordable.

Chefchaouen
MID-RANGE
Hotel Madrid, av Hassan II, tel: (039) 98 74 96, fax: (039) 98 74 98. Comfortable rooms with en-suite facilities and a convenient location.
Hôtel Parador, Place de Makhzen, tel: (039) 98 63 24, email: parador@iam.net.ma Attractive views, small pool. This hotel's restaurant is the best place to eat in Chefchaouen.

BUDGET
Hostal Gernika, 49 Calle Ibn Askar, Chefchaouen, tel/fax: (039) 98 74 34. Recently renovated guesthouse with choice of en-suite rooms or twin bed rooms with shared showers and WC. The roof terrace is a big plus.
Hôtel-Restaurant Tissemlal, 22 Rue Targui, tel: (039) 98 61 53. Very attractive and friendly accommodation (it has six rooms, three suites) with its own art gallery.

Tangier
LUXURY
El Pescador, 35 rue Allal-ben-Abdellah, tel: (039) 34 10 05. Refined seafood restaurant with attentive service.
Korsan, Hôtel el-Minzah, 85 Rue de la Liberté, tel: (039) 93 58 85. An attractive, atmospheric restaurant in Tangier's best hotel.
Restaurant Hamadi, 2 rue de la Kasbah, tel: (039) 93 45 14.

Tangier and the Mediterranean Coast at a Glance

Colourful traditional restaurant with musicians and entertainers.

MID-RANGE
Negresco, 20 Rue du Mexique, tel: (039) 93 80 97. Smart restaurant serving French and Moroccan cuisine in chic surroundings.
Saveurs de Poisson, Escallier Waller, Rue de la Liberté, tel: (039) 33 63 26. One of the best fish restaurants in town; simple and very good value.
Café de Paris, Place de France, no telephone. Tangier's best-known café is well named, with its French-style terrace and white-aproned waiters.
Porte du Nord, rue Ibn Rochd, tel: (039) 37 05 45. Old-fashioned elegance is the keynote at this café-patisserie which is one of the remnants of Tangier's golden age. The Porte du Nord does not serve full meals, but its mint tea or coffee is accompanied by a variety of sweet and sticky pastries and snacks.

BUDGET
Raihani, 10 Rue Ahmed Chaouki, tel: (039) 93 48 66. Good Moroccan food in a friendly restaurant in the New Town area.
San Remo, 15 Rue Ahmed Chaouki, tel: (039) 93 84 51. Fresh pasta is the speciality of this restaurant, as well as friendly service.

Chefchaouen
BUDGET
Casa Hassan, Hôtel-Restaurant Tissemlal, 22 Rue Targui, tel: (039) 98 61 53. Great Moroccan food and friendly multilingual service are the hallmarks of this owner-operated guesthouse and restaurant.

TOURS AND EXCURSIONS

Escorted tours from Tangier to sights around the region, including Chefchaouen, Tetouan, Asilah, Cap Spartel and the Grottes d'Hercule, can be arranged through larger hotels, including el-Minzah, or through the following agency:
Hit Voyages, 8 rue Khalid Ibn el Oualid, tel (039) 93 68 77. Helpful tour agency which arranges escorted trips around Tangier, the Mediterranean coast and the Rif region, and dinners with 'fantasia' shows of horsemanship and music.
Golf
Two good golf courses, which are open to visitors, are one of the legacies of the late King Hassan II, who was a keen golfer.

Tangier Royal Golf Club, Tangier, tel: (039) 94 44 84, fax: (039) 94 54 50.
Cabo Negro Royal Golf Club, Cabo Negro, tel: (039) 97 83 05.

USEFUL CONTACTS
Tourist Offices
Tangier
Office du Tourisme, 29 Boulevard Pasteur, tel: (039) 94 80 50.
Tetouan
Office du Tourisme, 30 Avenue Mohammed V, tel: (039) 96 44 07.
Syndicat d'Initiative et du Tourisme, Boulevard Hassan II, Residence Nakhil, tel: (037) 96 65 44.
Al Hoceima
Office du Tourisme, Ave. de Marrakech, tel: (039) 98 11 85.

Police, tel: 19.
Fire service, tel: 15.
Medical emergencies, tel: (039) 95 40 40.
Emergency pharmacy, 26 rue de Fes, Tangier, tel: (039) 93 26 19.
Emergency breakdown service, tel: 177.

TANGIER	J	F	M	A	M	J	J	A	S	O	N	D
AVERAGE TEMP. °F	64	66	68	72	75	77	79	79	77	75	68	61
AVERAGE TEMP. °C	18	19	20	22	24	25	26	26	25	24	20	16
HOURS OF SUN DAILY	6	7	8	9	11	12	12	12	12	12	8	7
RAINFALL in	2.5	2.5	2.5	2	1	0.2	0	0	0.3	1	2	2
RAINFALL mm	52	52	53	40	25	5	0	0	8	25	40	40
DAYS OF RAINFALL	15	15	20	10	8	1	0	0	2	10	10	12

3
Fez, Meknès and the Middle Atlas

South of the Rif massif, the mountains give way to rich plains that have made this region one of the heartlands of Moroccan civilization since antiquity. Guarded from interlopers by the natural rampart of the Rif, supplied by a fertile hinterland where villagers grow wheat, barley, grapes, citrus fruit, peaches and cotton, and watered by rivers and streams fed by the rains of the Rif and Middle Atlas, the imperial capitals of **Fez** and **Meknès** were the most prosperous and influential cities of medieval Morocco. They are places of great fascination for the visitor today, with superb monuments left by some of the land's most potent dynasties, and have absorbed inner cities that seem to have made few concessions to the 20th century, let alone the 21st.

Around these two cities is a patchwork of rolling **farmland** which, thanks to Morocco's mild climate, is verdant virtually year-round. To the south and west rises the chain of the **Middle Atlas**, descending on its eastern side to foothills and plains that gradually become more barren as they merge with the **Sahara**. The route through the Middle Atlas from Fez to Oujda, on the edge of the desert, is a spectacular one.

DON'T MISS

*** Fez el-Bali: the largest and most interesting medina quarter in Morocco.
*** Volubilis: ruins of an ancient Roman capital.
*** Fez el-Jedid: medieval royal capital, with its walls and palaces.
*** Gorges du Ziz: a spectacular desert canyon.
** Meknès: royal palaces, tombs and a fascinating, bustling medina.

FEZ

The capital of three of Morocco's great royal dynasties, Fez is both the **spiritual** and **cultural centre** of traditional Morocco and one of the country's most important cities, even in the 21st century. From the visitor's point of view, it is also one of the most striking of Moroccan cities,

Opposite: *The Bab Bou Jeloud is the busiest of the gateways which lead through the medieval walls of Fez's bustling medina.*

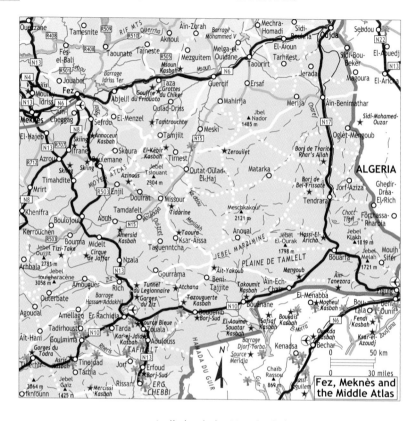

Fez, Meknès and the Middle Atlas

rivalled only by Marrakech for its immediate impact. Within its walls is the world's oldest, intact, continuously inhabited **medieval city**, and with a few relatively minor changes – such as a very basic electricity supply and some rudimentary plumbing – it seems to have changed little in more than 12 centuries.

Founded in 789AD, Fez became the first real **capital of Morocco** in 809, under Idriss I and Idriss II. Later dynasties, however, added monuments of their own. North of the original city, known as **Fez el-Bali**, the Merenid sultans built a new capital, **Fez el-Jedid**, and as usual the French built a new administrative and commercial town outside the walls of the old capital, southwest of Fez el-Jedid.

Opposite: *Fresh fruit and vegetables on sale in one of the Fez medina's many market streets.*

In sharp contrast to the old districts, this *ville nouvelle* is one of the most modern and Europeanized in Morocco, with smart shops and pavement cafés dotted along its main thoroughfare, Avenue Hassan II.

Since the mid-1990s, when Fez was declared a UNESCO World Heritage Site in recognition of its unique architectural and cultural treasures, a far-reaching conservation campaign has been taking place, guided by the government slum-clearance renovation agency, **Ader-Fez**, and supported by the Moroccan government, international organizations, and Moroccan companies and individuals. After several years of research, Ader-Fez has begun an ambitious programme to **train craftsmen** in traditional skills, **renovate homes** and **restore monuments** large and small. Among the more widespread signs of this renovation are the recently restored tile fountains, which – since the 11th and 12th centuries – have supplied the city with water from the **Oued Fez** (Fez River) and many other springs. New pipes have brought a clean, reliable water supply to 42 of these fountains all over the medina, and their beautiful tilework has been cleaned and restored.

Fez has a long history of craftsmanship, and some 30,000 **artisans** still utilize skills brought to the city by the early immigrants from Al-Andalus or Kairouan. Today, the city's wonderful potters, *zellij* tile-makers and tanners are legendary.

ZELLIJ

The multicoloured mosaics called *zellij* are typical of Moroccan decorative art, and are first seen in buildings dating from the 10th century AD. The craft was originally developed in Al-Andalus, where tiles called *azulejos* may be seen on many historic buildings. The earliest *zellij* work is in tones of **white** and **brown** but, as the art developed, more colours were added to the craftsman's palette, until by the 17th century many shades of **blue**, **green**, **yellow**, and **red** were in use. Patterns are highly **formalized**, and each style has its own name, range of colours and shapes of tile, all originally dictated by a *maalem*, or master artisan. With the restoration of several historic buildings, *zellij* skills are being preserved and revived.

Fez el-Bali ★★★

The oldest part of the city, Fez el-Bali stands on the east bank of the Oued Fez, which flows through the city centre. This old quarter – the largest **medina** in Morocco – is remarkably well preserved, thanks in part to the French General **Lyautey**, who decreed as early as 1913 that it

MEDINA GUIDES

Despite all steps taken to curb them, **Fez** still has some of the most aggressive and annoying *faux guides* (fake guides) of any Moroccan city. They tend to lurk around the **Bab Bou Jeloud** and other main gates, and will claim that it is impossible to find your way around the medina without a guide. This is untrue, but hiring an official guide from the tourist office can certainly aid and enhance your day's exploration.

should be protected from modernization. Most of its **streets** are too **narrow** for motor vehicles, and burdens are carried instead by heavily laden **mules**, **donkeys** and **human porters**.

Originally a modest **Berber** settlement, Fez grew rapidly after the arrival of 8000 families exiled from Al-Andalus in 818. These numbers were further increased by 300 families from Kairouan (Tunisia), who settled on the west bank in the district still known as **Kairaouine**.

Exploring the old medina can be a baffling experience, as there are more than **9000 alleys and lanes** that wind and wriggle through the medina, which like the old districts of all Moroccan cities, is a patchwork of overlapping **souks** specializing in different crafts and products. That said, a few days wandering through these streets will be one of the most memorable experiences of any visit to Morocco.

Bab Bou Jeloud ★★★

The Bab Bou Jeloud, midway along the southern wall, is among the most important and most impressive of the gates that pierce the walls of Fez el-Bali. Oddly, it is also the newest, and was only completed as recently as 1913. The minarets and crowded lanes framed in its

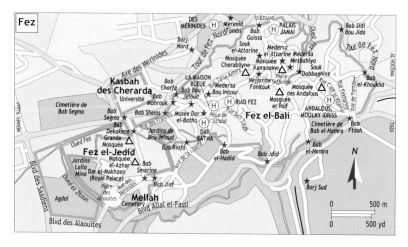

archway are an enticing picture. The gate is surrounded by **tilework** in gleaming blue (symbolizing Fez itself) and green, the colour of Islam.

Bab Mahrouk ★★

This imposing 12th-century gateway in the walls of the medina was the main entrance to the medieval town. Today it is the **main gateway** between the old medina area and the new residential suburbs outside the walls. Its ancient **stonework** has recently been restored to pristine glory.

Above: *The elaborately tiled Bab Bou Jeloud is the most impressive and important of the gates that lead into Fez's medina.*

Kairaouine Mosque and University ★★

In the centre of Fez el-Bali, the Kairaouine Mosque is the old city's most important landmark, while alongside stands the Kairaouine University, which is one of the most significant and highly regarded centres of **Islamic theological study** and teaching in the world. The complex is closed to non-Muslims, who may only glimpse the inner courtyard and prayer halls through the many gates that lead into the mosque precincts.

Medersa Mesbahiya ★

Currently undergoing renovation, this 14th-century *medersa* (Islamic school) is named after Aby Masbah, a Kairaouine scholar who was the first person to teach here, and is connected to the Kairaouine Mosque by a small sanctuary on Rue Boutouil. The Medersa Mesbahiya was partly ruined until a donation from the late King Hassan II made it possible to begin **restoration** work.

Medersa el-Attarine ★★

Close to the mosque on Rue Boutouil, behind a beautiful bronze door, this *medersa* was built by the Merenid ruler **Abu Said** in 1325, and its tiling, marble and alabaster,

---

HENNA, KOHL AND HARQUS

The powdered leaves of the henna plant are used to dye the hair (and sometimes also the feet and palms) a rich orange-red colour. Berber women were traditionally marked with tattoos on the face or hands to mark rites of passage such as puberty, marriage and childbirth, a practice that is less common today. Women still paint their hands and faces with elaborate traceries of a dye called **harqus**, made from ash and soot, on special occasions, and **kohl** (powdered galena) is used as eye make-up. Kohl bottles made of ebony, ivory, copper or inlaid wood make attractive souvenirs.

Above: *Brilliant, colourful tiles decorate the entrance to a* hammam *in Fez.*
Opposite: *Large vats of coloured dye in the famous tanneries of Fez.*

plasterwork and carved wooden decoration make this one of the most elegantly decorated *medersa* buildings in Morocco. It is open Monday–Thursday and Saturday–Sunday 08:00–17:00, Friday 08:00–12:00 and 14:00–17:00.

Souk el-Attarine ★★★

This market of shops and stalls cluttering Rue el-Attarine, leaving barely any room to pass, is the most colourful part of the medina, with bales, baskets and piles of **fruit** and **vegetables**, **herbs** and **spices**, as well as traditional **cosmetics**, including different kinds of henna, kohl, ghassoul (natural shampoo) and other perfumes and unguents.

Nejjarine Fondouk ★★

At the east end of Rue Talaa Kebira, the Nejjarine Fondouk was built as a **travellers' lodge** in the 17th century and was, in its day, an important commercial building. Like many other fondouks in Morocco, its original purpose was lost and it was taken over by craftsmen for use as **workshops**. It has recently been restored, and the renovation of the central area of the medina – known as Place Nejjarine – around the fondouk, with its square, fountain and carpentry shops, is one of the most striking examples of restoration and rehabilitation in the medina. Worth noting in particular are the elegant **cedar gateway** and **arcades** of the fondouk, which have also been restored to their former beauty. The fondouk is scheduled to become a **wood museum** where the worked wood of traditional architecture and the tools of this art will be exhibited, with a permanent display of carvings, furniture, and woodworking skills and tools.

Medersa Bou Inania ★★★

Built by the Sultan Bou Inan, and recently restored, the Medersa Bou Inania is a dazzling example of the heights of architectural and decorative refinement achieved in Fez under the Merenid sultans. Influenced by **Ottoman architecture** of the 14th century, its oriental influences distinguish it from all other *medersas* of the medina. The Bou Inania is still used as a **mosque** on Fridays. Also unique is its **water clock**, with its extraordinary, pre-clockwork mechanism. Designed in 1375, its purpose was to chime the hours of prayer. It was restored in 1990. Open daily 08:00–18:00.

Souk Dabbaghine ★★★

One of Fez's not-to-be-missed sights, Souk Dabbaghine (the **Tanners' Quarter**) is only about 50m (165ft) north of the Kairaouine – an unusual location considering that Islam sees tanning as an unclean activity, which should be located at a distance from any place of worship. In the morning, the **tanning pits** where leather is dyed are filled with dye in intense hues of crimson, purple, yellow and orange, in strong contrast with the white walls of surrounding buildings. Open dawn to dusk, Monday–Friday.

> ## LEO THE AFRICAN
>
> **Hassan al-Wazzan** was born in Granada in 1488. After the conquest of the city by Spain, his family fled to Fez, where Hassan was educated. He eventually became a prosperous merchant and traveller whose journeys took him across the Sahara to Timbuktu, east to Cairo. After making the pilgrimage to Mecca, he sailed to Tunis, where he was captured by Sicilian pirates in 1519. His gift for languages earned him an honoured post as **interpreter** to popes Leo X and Clement VII in their dealings with Ottoman and Arab potentates, and he remained in Rome until 1527, taking the name Leo Africanus (Leo the African) in honour of his papal patron. Returning to Fez, he wrote an account of his travels, the *Geographical History of Africa*, which offers a fascinating insight into the Mediterranean and Muslim world of the 16th century.

CARAVAN ROUTES

Until camels began to be bred in North Africa in the fourth century AD, trade between Morocco and the rich African kingdoms south of the Sahara was impossible. The first traders were Berbers, who exchanged **salt** (which the Africans lacked) for **gold** and **slaves** (which they had in plenty). The main Berber caravan routes from Morocco led from **Akka** through the oases of Taghaza and Taodeni to **Timbuktu** (in modern Mali) or from **Tafilalt** through the Touat Oasis to Timbuktu, **Agades**, or eastward through Libya to the **Siwa Oasis** in Egypt (where a Berber dialect is still spoken) and on to **Cairo**.

Merenid Tombs ★

Built for the Merenid sultans, these sepulchres outside the medina walls, on the south side of the Tour de Fez Nord ring road, have been pretty much reduced to rubble, with only a crumbling **arch** and tumbledown **walls** standing – and no trace of the lavish *zellij* mosaic that must once have adorned them. Open 24 hours.

Borj Nord ★

Also off Tour de Fez Nord, this small **fortress** built by Sultan Ahmed el-Mansour during the 16th century is now a **museum** of arms and armaments, mostly from the 18th–20th centuries. Open 08:00–12:00 and 14:30–18:00, Wednesday–Monday.

Fez el-Jedid ★★

Fez el-Jedid is known as **New Fez** and it is perhaps only here that a 13th-century walled city could be referred to as 'new', contrasting with its even more ancient neighbouring district, Fez el-Bali. Fez el-Jedid is an early example of a **planned city**, built by the Merenid

sultans in the 13th century, and, as a result, it is much easier to find your way around its streets than in the labyrinth of the older medina.

You can enter Fez el-Jedid either from Fez el-Bali via the Bou Jeloud Gardens and Bab Riafa, or from the new town by way of Boulevard Moulay Youssef. The heart of the Fez el-Jedid is the **Place des Alaouites**.

Dar el-Makhzen ★

In the very centre of Fez el-Jedid, on Place des Alaouites, the **Royal Palace** is the district's major landmark, with gold-plated doors on a tiled façade. The largest of the palaces still used by the royal family, it is – like all Morocco's royal palaces – closed to visitors.

The Mellah *

On the west side of Fez el-Jedid, the Mellah (former Jewish Quarter) has been abandoned by all but a tiny handful of Moroccan Jews, and is now mainly inhabited by migrants to the city from villages and rural areas. The area, nevertheless, still has some of its **distinctive architecture**: look out for upper storeys with their decorated **bay windows**

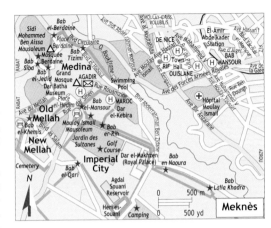

looking out onto the street. While their rights were traditionally respected inside the Mellah, Moroccan Jews were less free outside its walls: they were not permitted to wear shoes or ride a horse or donkey. One of the district's deconsecrated places of worship, the **Habanim Synagogue**, is presently being turned into a **museum of Jewish culture**.

Opposite: *On the skyline above Fez, the ruined Merenid tombs display a stark and eerie grandeur.*

MEKNÈS

Meknès is the product of one Moroccan ruler's dream and half a century of hard labour to create a new **imperial city**. Founded more than a thousand years ago, the city fell into the hands of the Almoravids in the 11th century, was taken by the Almohads in the 12th century and the Merenids in the 13th century and captured by the Wattasids in the 15th century. Finally, after the rise of the Alaouite dynasty, **Moulay Ismail**, the second Alaouite sultan (1672–1727), made it his **capital** and decreed the building of a vast imperial palace, a ring of ramparts pierced by massive gates, and a host of other monuments to his power. It was at least partly built by slave labour and as many as 3000 enslaved Christians and 30,000 convict labourers were employed in the building of its palaces, mosques, terraces, gardens, fountains, stables and souks. Like so many grandiose

> **WATER SELLERS**
>
> The *guerrab*, or water seller, of the Moroccan medina is less commonly seen in an era of piped or bottled water, but some *guerrab* may still be encountered in the medinas of **Fez** and **Marrakech**, in their colourful costume: scarlet *djellaba*, broad-brimmed, tasselled, red-and-yellow hat, and metal or leather water-carrier. The *guerrab* makes his living by carrying water from the fountain to sell by the cup to thirsty workmen or street traders.

Above: *In Meknès, the magnificent Bab el-Mansour is the most important of the portals leading into the medina through a ring of medieval battlements.*

projects, Moulay Ismail's great scheme was never entirely completed. After his death, his successors had different priorities, and after the city was partly demolished by an **earthquake**, his grandson Mohammed III decided to relocate the dynastic capital to Marrakech.

Meknès is, nevertheless, one of the most striking cities in Morocco, a place of grandiose **ruins** set among bustling **souks**, yet quieter than some of its rivals, and less visited by tourists than Tangier or Marrakech. The old part of the town is on the west bank of the Oued Boukfrane, which flows through the town, with the modern town on the east bank. A convenient point to start exploring the medina and the imperial city is **Place el-Hedim** at the southwest corner of the medina.

Dar el-Kebira ★★

The sprawling imperial city **palace complex**, built by Moulay Ismail, once contained two mosques and 20 pavilions for the sultan, his concubines and his inner circle. Not much remains of the original works but for the circuit of seemingly impregnable **walls** that once enclosed it. The ruins of the Dar el-Kebira complex are entered through the impressive **Bab el-Mansour** (Victory Gate) opposite Place el-Hedim – in fact, the gateway itself is probably the most impressive part of the entire complex. It is open 24 hours a day.

Dar el-Makhzen ★★

This official **royal residence and gardens**, southeast of the Bab el-Mansour, occupies most of the space inside the walls. A **golf course**, built at the behest of the late King Hassan II, occupies much of the rest. Dar el-Makhzen is closed to the public.

OASES

The oases of the desert fringes occur naturally where underground watercourses, fed by the rain and snow of the Atlas mountains, come to the surface. **Palm trees** flourish, and provide shade where **fruit and vegetable gardens** can be cultivated. Most oases were, for many centuries, virtually self-sufficient, and inhabitants traded with nomad pastoralists and desert-crossing caravans for goods they could not produce themselves. Today, large areas are given over to the commercial cultivation of **date palms**.

Heri es-Souani **

This complex of **stables** and **granaries**, built into the city walls in the southwest corner of the imperial city, gives some idea of the sheer scale of Moulay Idriss's planning. Its walls are 3m (10ft) thick and its many chambers were intended to store fodder for the 12,000 horses stabled next to it. From the terrace above there are **views** over the **Agdal Souani Reservoir**, a 4m-deep (13ft) artificial lake, with an area of 4ha (10 acres), which provided water for the palace and its gardens. From here, water ran through an ingenious system of **channels** to cool the stables and palace. Open 09:00–12:00 and 15:00–18:00 daily.

Moulay Ismail Mausoleum ***

The mausoleum of Moulay Ismail is as opulent as even he could have wished, with **fountains** sparkling in a tiled courtyard, carved marble and delicately inlaid and carved **woodwork**, and thick Meknès **rugs** muffling the sound of footsteps on its flagstoned floor. Open daily 09:00–12:00 and 15:00–18:00, but open only to Muslims on Friday mornings.

The Medina

Meknès's medina area is a lot less concerned with tourism than those of Tangier, Marrakech or Fez. There are plenty of **shops** selling carpets and other handicrafts, but they are well outnumbered by those serving the everyday needs of local people.

Dar Batha Museum **

On the north side of the Place el-Hedim, the **Jamai Palace** was the seat of the Jamai family, a dynasty of Meknès notables, two of whom became *wazirs* (ministers) to the 19th-century sultan, Hassan I. Housed in the Jamai Palace, Dar Batha Museum (the Museum of

Below: *Raw wool is beaten before being spun, dyed and woven into rugs and carpets.*

HAMMAMS

An age-old feature of most medinas is the *hammam*. Though often associated with the Islamic world, these **public steam baths** were a feature of the Roman and Byzantine worlds too. Comprising a sequence of domed chambers – disrobing room and pool, cool and warm rooms and, finally, the steam room – the *hammam* is virtually identical to the baths of the Roman era. With the advent of Islam and its emphasis on ritual cleanliness, however, the *hammam* became a central part of religious as well as social life. Strictly segregated by gender, the *hammam* is a very important meeting place especially for Moroccan women.

Moroccan Arts) is worth visiting for the **building** alone. A good example of a 19th-century Moroccan palace, it has a grand *koubba* (reception room) and state rooms. Exhibits include wonderful silver and amber jewellery, pottery, richly coloured rugs and carpets, and fine woodwork, including the *minbar* (pulpit) from a 17th-century mosque. Outside is an attractive **garden**, where you may like to catch your breath before diving into the bedlam of the medina. Open 08:30–12:00 and 14:30–18:30 Wednesday–Monday.

MOULAY IDRISS

Overlooked by the unique **cylindrical minaret** of the Khiber *medersa* in the upper town, Moulay Idriss is named after the country's most venerated figure, the religious leader and ruler who is credited with founding the first Moroccan state. Much smaller and quieter than Fez or even Meknès, it explodes into life in August each year when the annual *moussem* (religious festival) attracts thousands of **pilgrims** from the countryside and from all over Morocco. Built on two crags on the slopes of the 950m (3000ft) Jebel Zerhoun, 24km (15 miles) north of Meknès, the city looks over the valley of the Oued Khouman.

VOLUBILIS (OULILI)

The major city of Rome's North African province of Mauretania, Volubilis was built some 14km (9 miles)

west of Moulay Idriss and became the capital city of the kings of Mauretania. Under the **Romans**, it reached its heyday in the 2nd and 3rd centuries, when it was a major trading city as well as the seat of the procurators (the governors) of Mauretania Tingitana. Its main commerce was in **oil**, but it also pandered to the Roman taste for exotic **wild animals**, supplying lions, leopards and elephants as prestige pets and for gladiatorial contests in the Roman arena. Volubilis was abandoned by the Romans some time during the late 4th or the early 5th centuries and gradually fell into ruin, but people continued to live here until the 18th century, when Moulay Ismail's masons discovered it as a handy source of precut **marble** and pulled down most of its buildings to use the stone in the construction of imperial Meknès.

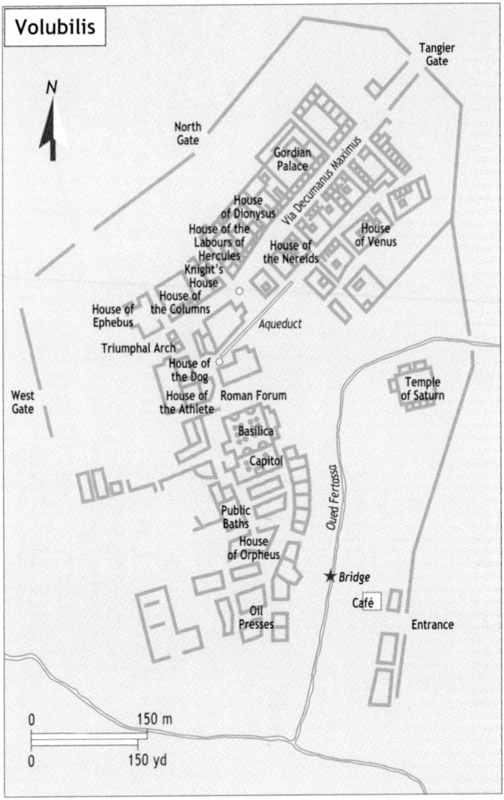

Via Decumanus Maximus **

The entrance to Volubilis is on the south side of the site, but it is best to walk 500m (1640ft) north to the Via Decumanus Maximus, the street that was once the city's main thoroughfare, on which most of the best-preserved and restored buildings stand. Before you reach this, however, detour left to look at the **basilica**, with its tall arches and the roofless columns of the capitol and Roman forum.

Volubilis

N

Tangier Gate

North Gate

Gordian Palace

Via Decumanus Maximus

House of Dionysus
House of the Labours of Hercules
Knight's House
House of the Nereids
House of Venus
House of the Columns
House of Ephebus
Aqueduct
Triumphal Arch
House of the Dog
House of the Athlete
Roman Forum
Temple of Saturn
Basilica
Capitol
Oued Fertassa
Public Baths
House of Orpheus
Bridge
Café
Oil Presses
Entrance
West Gate

0   150 m
0   150 yd

Triumphal Arch **

Further on, the most important and prominent landmark is the Triumphal Arch, at the southwest end of the Via Decumanus Maximus, a looming structure of sandstone blocks built in 217AD to honour **Emperor Caracalla**. French archaeologists rebuilt it in the 1930s, and further (and more accurate) restoration took place in the 1960s.

Opposite: *The Triumphal Arch is the most important and prominent landmark at Volubilis, the ruined former capital of the Roman province of Mauretania.*

Above: *Red mud-brick kasbahs rise above the palm plantations of the Dadès Valley, with the peaks of the Haut Atlas in the background.*

Roman Villas ★★

Stretching uphill from the Triumphal Arch are the ruins of **villas**, worth seeing for their fine **mosaic floors** and public buildings. Among the most striking of mosaic floors are those of the **House of Orpheus**, where coloured tiles depict scenes from classical mythology; the **House of Dionysus**, with its mosaic depicting the four seasons; and the **House of Ephebus**, with its triclimium (banqueting room) appropriately decorated with a mosaic of Bacchus, god of wine and celebration.

THE MIDDLE ATLAS

The foothills of the Middle Atlas begin to rise from the central plains about 64km (40 miles) from Fez. The slopes are in many places thickly **wooded** with cedar and pine and are watered by numerous streams and rivers. Higher up, conifer forests give way to arid limestone slopes. The N6 highway leads northeast from Fez, through the **Taza Pass**, which divides the Middle Atlas from the Rif range, to **Oujda**. The R503 route south from Fez runs through the Sefrou valley and the medieval fortified town of Sefrou, while the N8 follows the equally attractive valley route through the Middle Atlas from Meknès. The best time to travel this route is in **spring**, when the mountain slopes form a green backdrop to a blaze of red, yellow and purple **flowers**.

TAZA

Commanding the Taza Gap – the only pass through the eastern Rif and Middle Atlas between the central plains and the sea – Taza was once a **strategic citadel**, as its impressive ramparts still suggest.

The Medina and City Walls ★★

Built by the Almohads during the 12th century, the walls of the medina were added to (and battered down) by successive rulers and are gradually crumbling. From the **Bab er-Rih** (Gate of the Wind) on the northern wall, you can walk most of the way around the ramparts – worth it just for the view. Inside the medina are two 12th-century

mosques (neither of which is open to non-Muslims), and the **Berber souks** (right in the centre of the medina) are colourful places in which to bargain for rugs woven by mountain villagers.

Gouffre du Friouato ★★★

About 16km (10 miles) south of Taza on the route 4822, this **huge grotto** is the largest in North Africa. Discovered in 1935, it has not yet been fully charted. You need your own torch and a good head for heights to explore it – the visit involves descending more than 700 very steep steps – but the bizarre rock formations in the lower chambers make the climb worthwhile. Allow at least 4–5hrs. Open 08:00–18:00 daily.

OUJDA

East of Taza, the N6 highway follows the valley of the Oued Msoun through Taourirt to the dusty, sleepy town of Oujda on the Algerian border. Oujda may become more lively if and when the **border crossing** (closed since the early 1990s) reopens, but for most visitors it is just a peaceful way station en route south. From here, the N17 highway runs 368km (230 miles) through the desert fringes to Figuig, Morocco's outpost in the Sahara.

FIGUIG

Like Oujda, Figuig is really only for those for whom the desert holds a deep fascination. It is surrounded by **palm** plantations of around 10,000 trees, but there is little else to see and there are no good hotels or places to eat.

SEFROU

Sefrou, 28km (17 miles) south of Fez at an altitude of 850m (2800ft), is a pleasantly uncommercialized walled town at the mouth of the gorge of the Oued Aggai. It has no outstanding sights, but its small **medina** is worth a visit – it is much more hassle-free than those of Fez or Meknès.

EUGENE DELACROIX

The Western world owes many of its **exotic images of Morocco** to Eugene Delacroix, the **painter** who accompanied the French mission led by the Comte de Mornay in 1832. Delacroix was dazzled by the **light**, the **people** and the **places**, and the voyage was a major influence on his work throughout his life – he filled **seven albums** with sketches and studies, which were later transformed into his famed paintings of Moroccan feasts, weddings, dancers and musicians. Many of these can be seen in the Louvre in Paris and in other important international art collections.

Below: *Landscapes like these are typical of the Moyen Atlas, one of the four major mountain ranges which have shaped Morocco's climate, culture and history.*

IFRANE

For most of the year, Ifrane – about 64km (40 miles) south of Fez – is no more than a place to stop and stretch your legs, but in Morocco's short (and not very reliable) ski season, it is popular with people from Casablanca and Rabat taking a weekend **winter-sports** break. The resort, with its incongruous Alpine-style chalets, is surrounded by forests.

THE ZIZ GORGES AND THE TAFILALT

As you descend from the Middle Atlas to the eastern plains, the landscape becomes steadily harsher and more **arid**, with patches of palm trees growing along the region's streams and rivers. Heading south from Ifrane, the N13 highway passes through the unexciting town of Midelt through the superb Gorges du Ziz and the valley of the Oued Ziz to Er Rachidia and the oases of Tafilalt Valley, evocative of every desert romance ever filmed.

Gorges du Ziz ★★★

Between the small town of Rich, 320km (200 miles) southeast of Ifrane and Er Rachidia, the Ziz Gorges stretch for 20km (12 miles) of red and ochre **rock walls** – sculpted by eons of wind, sand and extreme heat and cold – rising steeply from the winding river bed.

Below: *Kasbahs and ksours like these in the Ziz Valley are gradually becoming things of the past as concrete and brick replace traditional clay-and-timber construction.*

Addakhil Dam and Lake ★

South of the Ziz Gorges, the Oued Ziz broadens into an incongruous **artificial lake** behind the Addakhil Dam.

ER RACHIDIA

Er Rachidia, a garrison town built by the French, is far from fascinating, but does have acceptable accommodation and restaurants, and is the main regional **transport hub** for travel to all points of the compass. From Er Rachidia, you could take highway N10 south-west to the Dadès Valley,

Ouarzazate and the Drâa Valley; you could head east to Figuig on route N10; or, most rewardingly, continue to the south along the Ziz Valley.

Source Bleue ★★

The Source Bleue (Blue Spring) is a natural desert spring and **swimming hole** some 23km (14 miles) south of Er Rachidia, and beckons irresistibly to anyone travelling past on route N13.

THE TAFILALT VALLEY

The Tafilalt Valley, with its (estimated) **one million palm trees** watered by the headwaters of the Oued Ziz, can be explored from either Erfoud or Rissani.

Erfoud ★

Erfoud, 98km (60 miles) south of Er Rachidia on the banks of the Oued Ziz, is the gateway to the remote Tafilalt oasis region. Like Er Rachidia, it was built by the French as a **garrison town** to pacify the restive tribes of the Tafilalt and is no architectural gem, with its buildings laid out in a grid of streets around two main avenues.

Rissani ★★

Rissani, in the heart of the oasis region, is built on the site of Sijilmassa, once the terminus for one of the most important trans-Saharan **caravan routes**, but sacked and destroyed by the French during the 19th century. It holds an interesting **market** three times a week on a Sunday, Tuesday and Thursday.

The Erg Chebbi ★★★

About 50km (31 miles) south of Erfoud, the small settlement of Merzouga's only claim to fame is the surrounding region of **red sand dunes** known as the Erg Chebbi. This wonderfully romantic landscape is a unique taste of what the deep desert can be like, as it is the only region of real sand dunes in Morocco – most of Morocco's desert territory comprises seemingly endless flat expanses of sand, gravel and low rocky hills.

Above: *Red sand dunes at Erg Chebbi offer a taste of the deep Sahara Desert.*

MOROCCAN SWITZERLAND

With its cedars and pine woods, modern chalets and holiday apartments, **Ifrane** has been nicknamed the 'Moroccan Switzerland', though in fact it looks like any northern European suburb. Founded in 1929 as a resort for French colonialists, it now attracts wealthier Moroccans and has both a Royal Palace and a prestigious university.

Fez, Meknès and the Middle Atlas at a Glance

BEST TIMES TO VISIT

Apr–May and Sep–Dec. In summer, Fez and Meknès become very hot, and temperatures can pass 40°C (74°F) before noon. The desert fringes can be even hotter.

GETTING THERE

By Air: British Airways (www.ba.com) flies several times weekly from London Gatwick. Ryanair (www.ryanair.com) flies several times weekly from London Luton. **By Road:** Buses to Fez and Meknès from Tangier, Casablanca, Rabat, Marrakech and points south; and to Oujda and Erfoud. Long-haul taxis also operate on main routes. **By Rail:** Trains from Fez and Meknès to Tangier, Rabat and Casablanca.

GETTING AROUND

In Fez and Meknès, use **taxis** rather than urban buses. **Horse-drawn carriages** can also be hired by the day or hour. **Four-wheel-drive vehicles** (with driver) can be chartered to explore the Tafilalt and the Erg Chebbi from Erfoud and Er Rachidia.

WHERE TO STAY

Fez
LUXURY
La Maison Bleue, 2 Place de l'Istiqlal, Batha, tel: (035) 63 60 52, www.maisonbleue.com Lovely Moroccan townhouse with a glass-roofed courtyard, stylish décor and furnishing, six suites with four-poster beds.

Jnan Palace Fez, Avenue Ahmed Chaouki, tel: (035) 65 22 30, fax: (035) 65 19 17, e-mail: jp@fesnet.net.ma Superb, luxurious, five-star in the city centre next to the medina, with 7ha (17-acre) gardens and a lovely pool.

MID-RANGE
Hôtel Palais Jamai, Bab Guissa, tel: (035) 63 43 31, fax: (035) 63 50 96, www.sofitel.com This hotel (part of the French Sofitel chain) is on the outskirts of the medina, with restaurants, pool and splendid architecture. **Riad Fez**, 5 Darb Benslimane Zerbtana, tel: (035) 94 76 10, www.riadfes.com Opened in January 2001, this lovely riad (*see* page 123) has 16 suites, authentic décor and a pool.

BUDGET
Riad al Bartel, 21 Rue Sournas, tel/fax: (035) 63 70 53, www.riadalbartal.com Unprepossessing outside, this affordable French-owned riad in a 1930s mansion has five suites and is decorated in traditional Fezzi colours, tiles and stucco.

Meknès
LUXURY
Hôtel Transatlantique, Rue el-Meriniyine, tel: (035) 52 50 50, fax: (035) 52 00 57. The best hotel in Meknès, this medium-sized establishment has a location overlooking the medina, a swimming pool, choice of restaurants and tennis courts.

MID-RANGE
Hôtel Rif, Rue d'Accra, tel: (035) 52 25 91, fax: (035) 52 44 28. Slightly shabby four-star in the new town, with a pool.

BUDGET
Hôtel Bab Mansour, 38 Rue Emir Abdelkader, tel: (035) 52 52 39, fax: (035) 51 07 41. Simple, basic and very cheap.

Erfoud
LUXURY
Hôtel Salam, Route du Rissani, tel: (035) 57 66 65, fax: (035) 57 64 26. Best four-star in Erfoud, with own restaurant, bar, sauna and other facilities.

MID-RANGE
Hôtel Kasbah Tizimi, Route du Tinerhir, tel: (035) 57 61 79, fax: (035) 57 73 75, www.kasbahtizimi.com Excellent value, pleasant courtyard and comfortable rooms, very near town centre.

BUDGET
Hôtel Tafilalet, Avenue Moulay Ismail, tel: (035) 57 65 35, www.grouptafilalet.ma Comfortable three-star with pool. Request one of the newer rooms with a balcony.

WHERE TO EAT

Fez
LUXURY
La Medaille, 25 re Laarbi-Karghat, tel: (035) 62 01 83. Surroundings a bit bland, but serves a good array of local and international dishes.

Fez, Meknès and the Middle Atlas at a Glance

Les Remparts de Fes, 2 Arset Jiar Bab el Guissa, tel: (035) 63 74 15. Musicians and belly dancers entertain diners at this grand, very popular restaurant. **Restaurant l'Ambra**, 47 rte d'Immouzer, tel: (035) 64 16 87. One of the most expensive eating places in Fez, but serves superb Moroccan food in sybaritic surroundings. **Restaurant Zagora**, 5 Bd Mohammed V, tel: (035) 94 06 86. This chic restaurant serves excellent pastilla, along with international cooking. Better than average wine list.

MID-RANGE
Ryad Mabrouka, Derb il Miter, Talaa Kibeera, tel: (035) 63 63 45. Moroccan and mainstream European menu, very good value. Evenings only, reservations recommended. **Restaurant Marrakech**, 11 rue Omar el Mokhtar, tel: (035) 62 25 27. This good grill restaurant in the new town also serves excellent Moroccan dishes such as *tajine* and pastilla.

BUDGET
La Kasbah, 18 Bab Boujeloud, tel: (035) 74 15 33. Affordable restaurant has a great location at the entrance to the medina, with views from its terraces. No alcohol.
Sicilia, 4 ave Abdellah Chefchaouni, tel: (035) 62 52 65. In the new town, this is a pleasant and inexpensive sandwich bar.

Meknès
MID-RANGE
Collier de la Colombe, 67 Rue Driba, tel: (035) 55 50 41. Good views; fine traditional dishes and international menu; value for money.

BUDGET
Restaurant Métropole, 11 Rue Charif Idrissi, tel: (035) 52 56 68. Extremely cheap and excellent value, with a choice of filling Moroccan dishes such as *tajines*.

Erfoud
MID-RANGE
Hôtel Kasbah Tizimi, Route du Tinerhir, tel: (035) 57 61 79, fax: (035) 57 73 75. The best restaurant in town, with reasonably priced Moroccan and some international dishes.

TOURS AND EXCURSIONS

Tours and excursions to Marrakech, Casablanca and Rabat, and also into the villages of the Middle Atlas, High Atlas and the oases, are offered by a range of tour and travel agencies in both Fez and Marrakech.

USEFUL CONTACTS

Tourist Offices
Fez
Tourist Board, Place de la Resistance, tel: (035) 62 34 60, fax: (035) 65 43 70.
Tourist Information Office, Place Mohammed V, tel: (035) 62 47 69.

Meknès
Regional Tourist Office, 27 Batha l'Istiqlal, tel: (035) 52 4426, fax: (035) 51 60 46.
Tourist Information Office, Esplanade de la Foire, tel: (035) 52 01 91.

Oujda
Regional Tourist Office, Place du 16 Aout 1953, tel: (035) 68 56 31, fax: (035) 68 90 89.
Tourist Information Office, Place du 16 Aout 1953, tel: (035) 68 97 72.

Er Rachidia
Regional Tourist Office, Bd Moulay Ali Cherif, tel: (035) 57 0944, fax: (035) 57 09 43.

Ifrane
Regional Tourist Office, Place du Syndicat, tel: (035) 56 68 21.

FEZ	J	F	M	A	M	J	J	A	S	O	N	D
AVERAGE TEMP. °F	64	66	68	72	77	88	95	95	88	77	70	61
AVERAGE TEMP. °C	18	19	20	22	25	31	35	35	31	25	21	16
HOURS OF SUN DAILY	6	7	8	9	11	12	12	12	12	12	8	7
RAINFALL in	2.5	2.5	2.5	2	1	0.2	0	0	0.3	1	2	2
RAINFALL mm	52	52	53	40	25	5	0	0	8	25	40	40
DAYS OF RAINFALL	15	15	20	10	8	1	0	0	2	10	10	12

4
Rabat, Casablanca and Surrounds

Rabat, Morocco's **official capital** and seat of government, lies approximately 240km (150 miles) south of Tangier, strategically sited on the Atlantic coast at the mouth of the Oued Bou Regreg. Although **Rabat** is the home of the country's parliament, the main official residence of the king and the base of all government ministries, it is – in commercial and industrial terms – less important than Casablanca. About 80km (50 miles) south of Rabat and also on the Atlantic, **Casablanca**, the **former colonial capital**, is still unchallenged as Morocco's largest city and its commercial and industrial hub. Both cities are growing rapidly and, in not too many years, are likely to merge into one long coastal conurbation, also absorbing the industrial port and would-be beach resort, **Mohammedia**, which lies between the two main cities.

Rabat and Casablanca each represent a different and much more modern and cosmopolitan face of Morocco than cities such as Fez, Marrakech and Meknès. Casablanca, especially, is a creation of the European colonial era and, as such, is really a product of the 19th and 20th centuries. Rabat has older antecedents and has had its moments of glory over the centuries, but like Casablanca it is mainly a modern city.

That said, both cities have their points of **historic** interest as well as introducing the visitor to aspects of **modern** Morocco. For many visitors arriving by air, Casablanca will be the gateway to Morocco, and Rabat has the cachet that goes with being a royal capital.

Don't Miss

*** Hassan II Mosque:** grandiose monument to a 20th-century ruler.
**** Kasbah des Oudaias:** 12th-century citadel guarding the city of Rabat.
**** Tour Hassan:** 12th-century minaret.
**** Salé's Medina:** whitewashed houses, mosques and craft shops.

Opposite: *The King Hassan II Mosque is Casablanca's most grandiose landmark. It is open to non-Muslims at certain times.*

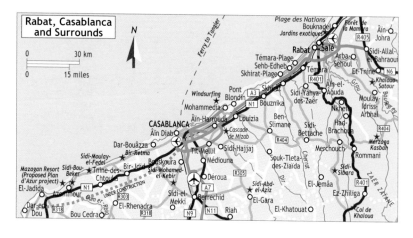

BARBARY CORSAIRS

During the 16th and 17th centuries, the Western Mediterranean became a theatre of **marine warfare** between the Spanish empire and its allies and the navies of the Ottoman Empire, whose Sultan, in Constantinople, had become ruler of all Islam. The galley fleets of the Muslim corsairs of Tunis, Algiers and other North African ports on the 'Barbary coast' raided far and wide – as did the ships of Spain, Venice and Genoa – while the infamous **Sallee Rovers** sailed even further afield, raiding as far north as Iceland. The activities of these pirates and slave raiders were not finally curbed until the early decades of the 19th century.

Neither Rabat nor Casablanca is dependent on tourism and, as a result, the relentless hustle and salesmanship that are encountered in the medinas of Marrakech and Tangier are pretty much absent.

Between Casablanca and Rabat lies a stretch of sandy coastline with a scattering of small to medium-sized **beach resorts** – Harhoura, Témara, Sables d'Or and Skhirat – that cater mainly to city residents wishing to get out of town for weekends and holidays. These beaches are not very impressive: if sun, sea and sand are the most important aspects of your holiday, Morocco has far better beach resorts at Essaouira and Agadir.

As you drive into the urban area comprising Rabat and Salé, do not be deterred by what may appear at first glance to be a modern and rather dull city. Rabat has a portfolio of relics of a more distant and illustrious past, a pleasant climate and a very attractive mixture of old and new, epitomized by the striking contrast between the more modern city of **Rabat** and its neighbour, old-fashioned **Salé**. Rabat proper is situated on the south bank of the Oued Bou Regreg, with the white harbour city of Salé (at one time the home port of the notorious Sallee Rovers) facing it across the river. Though the cities have merged into one conurbation, the **historic centre** of each has a character of its own.

The **Romans** founded a city called Sala Colonia on a site south of modern Rabat, at what was then the mouth of the river – a river that has, due to silting and the tidal action of the Atlantic, changed its course significantly over centuries. After the departure of the Romans, it became a **Berber** enclave, but as the course of the river changed it was eventually abandoned, and a new river-mouth settlement sprang up on the site of modern Salé. During the 12th century, the city fell under the sway of the Almohad dynasty and the **fortified kasbah** was constructed on the south bank of the river. With the death of Al-Mansour, the greatest of the Almohads, Rabat and Salé dwindled in importance. Recovery came during the 17th century when an influx of Andalusian Muslim immigrants, expelled from Spain by King Philip III, settled in both Rabat and Salé.

This was the heyday of the **corsairs** – known in Europe as the Sallee Rovers – and, for a while in the early part of the century (1627–39), the twin towns even became an independent outlaw state, the Republic of **Bou Regreg**. They were eventually brought under the sway of the Alaouite sultans, but continued with their piratical activities until the early 19th century, when piracy all along the 'Barbary Coasts' of Morocco, Tunisia and Algeria was finally suppressed by the navies of the Western powers. Rabat became the official capital of the French protectorate declared in 1912, and continued to be the seat of **residence** and of the **royal family** after independence in 1956.

RABAT
The Medina **

Rabat's walled medina, which dates from the 17th century, faces the Atlantic to the north and from its eastern wall looks across the Bou Regreg estuary to Salé. The southern rampart forms the boundary between the medina and the new town.

> **COUSCOUS**
>
> Couscous is Moroccan cooking's answer to rice, pasta or potatoes. The bulk **carbohydrate** over which dozens of different sauces and *tajines* are served, couscous is the crushed grain of **boulghour**, or bulgur wheat, usually steamed or boiled and often also served cold in salad dishes.

Below: *The picturesque Kasbah des Oudaias in Rabat dates from the 13th century.*

Kasbah des Oudaias ★★

Entered through the Bab Oudaia, the kasbah occupies the promontory between the medina, the ocean and the river. It is named after the garrison of Oudaya Bedouin mercenaries sent by **Sultan Moulay Ismail** to defend the town from Berber tribesmen during the 13th century. Built by the Almohads in the late 12th and early 13th centuries,

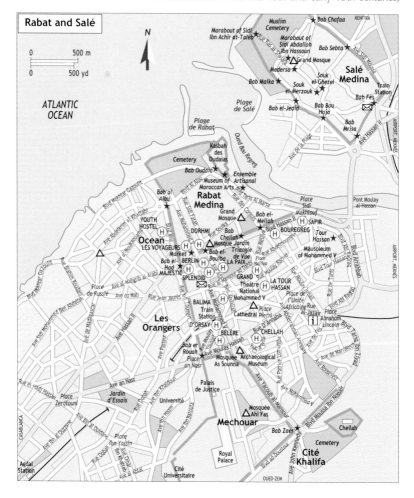

its **walls** were strengthened
between 1666 and 1672 –
during the reign of Moulay
Rachid – and are some 2.5m
(8ft) thick and from 8m (26ft) to
9.5m (31ft) in height. Within
these massive ramparts, the
architecture of its houses clearly
shows the influence of the
Muslim exiles from Al-Andalus
who settled here and revived
the city's fortunes. In the centre

of the kasbah is the **Jamaa al-Atiq**, the oldest **mosque** in
Rabat, dating from 1150. The kasbah is open 24 hours
daily, but the mosque is not open to non-Muslims.

Above: *The Tour Hassan,
intended as a monument
to Yacoub al-Mansour,
was never completed.*

Museum of Moroccan Arts ★
Housed in a small palace built for Sultan Moulay Ismail
in the 17th century, the museum comprises displays of
traditional **costumes** and Moroccan **musical
instruments**. Open 09:00–12:00 and 15:00–17:00,
Monday–Friday (until 18.00 June–September).

Archaeological Museum ★★★
The museum, at 23 Rue al Brihi, should not be missed by
those with an interest in Morocco's **Roman** and historic
past. Its collection includes marble busts, pottery
and bronze ware from the Roman cities of **Lixus** and
Volubilis, and from **Sala Colonia**, near present-day
Rabat. The museum is open 09:00–12:00 and
14:00–17:00, Wednesday–Monday.

Tour Hassan and Mausoleum of Mohammed V ★★
This 44m (144ft) tower, on a site overlooking the river at
the northern end of Boulevard Abi Radraq, is Rabat's
main historic landmark. The tower was to be the minaret
of a grand mosque, intended as a monument to **Yacoub
al-Mansour**, under whom the Almohad dynasty reached
its peak. Al-Mansour died in 1199, just four years after
work began on the mosque, and his successors were too

> **TRADITIONAL DRESS**
>
> For many working-class
> Moroccan men and women,
> the *djellaba*, a long, hooded
> garment, is everyday wear.
> The *djellaba* may be made of
> wool for winter or cotton for
> hotter weather and is one of
> the world's most practical
> and comfortable garments.
> Rif women often wear the
> *fouta*, a colourful long skirt
> in red and white stripes, and
> in cold weather or at night
> Berber villagers wear the
> *hendira*, a striped blanket
> worn as a cloak.

Above: *The Grand Mosque in Salé is the most important landmark within the walls of the Salé medina.*

busy feuding to finish it. What now remains is the **pillar** and 2–3m (6–10ft) **columns** indicating the planned site of the mosque. Next to the tower is the **tomb** of Morocco's first post-independence sultan (and the grandfather of the present king), **Mohammed V.** The tomb is an interesting and opulent fusion of modern and traditional Moroccan architectural techniques. Open 09:00–12:00 and 15:00–18:00, daily except Friday.

Chellah ★★

At the junction of Avenue Yacoub al-Mansour and Boulevard ad-Doustour, the Chellah, or **necropolis**, of the Merenids stands on the site of the Roman settlement of Sala Colonia. Completed in the early 14th century, the necropolis is evocative of a vanished dynasty. The **tombs** are overgrown by shrubs and creepers, wild birds are abundant, and the eels and terrapins that live in the walled pool fed by a natural spring are regarded as harbingers of good luck by the locals, who also believe that the Muslim saints whose tombs stand nearby can restore fertility to childless women. Open 08:30–17:00 daily (18:00 in summer).

SALÉ

The Medina ★★

Cross the Oued Bou Regreg by the Pont Moulay al-Hassan to enter the whitewashed medina of Salé through the **Bab Bou Haja**, the main gate through its southwest wall. Salé is much more atmospheric than Rabat, and its medina is actually larger than its new quarter – unlike its larger neighbour, where the new town dwarfs the old medina area. There are several **souks** within Salé's medina: the most interesting to visit are the **Souk el-Merzouk** – a street of textile-weavers, silversmiths and basket makers – and the **Souk el-Ghezel**, the medina's wool market.

STORKS

The stork is **Morocco's national bird**, and huge flocks can be seen passing through on their spring and autumn migrations, arriving in spring from the southern Sahara. Large numbers nest in Morocco, building messy, wheel-shaped nests of twigs and reeds on houses and disused buildings as well as in trees. Two species – the **black stork** and **white stork** – can be seen, patrolling river banks, ponds, marshes and fields in search of a variety of prey including frogs, fish and fledgling birds.

Grand Mosque and Medersa ★★

The Grand Mosque is the Salé medina's most important sight and is a fine example of religious architecture of the Merenid era. Built in 1333 in the reign of Abu al-Hassan Ali, its exterior is decorated with coloured **tiles** and finely carved **plaster work**. The mosque is closed to non-Muslims but you can visit the attached *medersa*, which is no longer used by scholars. From the roof, you have a good panoramic **view** of Salé's medina and across the river to the kasbah and medina of Rabat and the Tour Hassan. Open 09:00–12:00 and 15:00–18:00 daily.

Marabout of Sidi Abdallah Ibn Hassoun ★

The small white *marabout* (shrine or tomb) of Sidi Abdallah Ibn Hassoun stands just north of the Grand Mosque on Rue Ras as-Shajara, and is the focus of an annual pilgrimage and festival. The Sidi died in 1604 (his birth date is not known, but is believed to have been in the first quarter of the previous century). He made the perilous pilgrimage to **Mecca** and to other Islamic holy places, and is not only the revered guardian of Salé, but is regarded as a protector of pilgrims and travellers, including sailors and fishermen. The shrines of such Muslim saints are known variously as *marabouts*, *koubbas* or *zaouias*.

Muslim Cemetery and Marabout of Sidi Ibn Achir ★★

The large Muslim cemetery, with its turban-crowned tombs and inscriptions of Koranic verses, occupies an area of almost 1km^2 ($^1/_3$ sq mile) between the old town and the sea and is a reminder that Salé was once a bigger, more important place. At the western end of Rue Ras as-Shajara, in the middle of the cemetery, stands the shrine of **Sidi Ibn Achir at-Taleb**, another Muslim holy man and poet known as 'at-Taleb' ('the healer') because of his reputed posthumous ability to cure the sick.

WINE AND ROMANCE

Around 100km (62 miles) inland from Azemmour lies **Boulouane**, where the grapes for Morocco's best rosé wine grow in vineyards overlooked by the ruined **Kasbah de Boulouane**, on the banks of the Oum er-Rbia river. The kasbah is said to have been built by **Sultan Moulay Ismail** in 1710, and it and the palace within were given by him to the family of a local beauty who became his favourite wife. When she died, he destroyed the kasbah in his grief.

Below: *Finely made silver- and brassware can be found in the various souks of Rabat and Salé.*

AROUND RABAT AND SALÉ

Plage de Rabat and Plage de Salé ★

The two somewhat grubby urban **beaches** face each other across the mouth of the Bou Regreg. For better, cleaner bathing, head north to **Plage des Nations** (6km/ 4 miles north of Rabat) or **Mehdiya Plage** (2km/1 mile beyond Plage des Nations).

Mamora Forest ★

This 134,000ha (330,000-acre) forest of thinly scattered **cork oak** and **eucalyptus** trees is a boon to birdwatchers and nature lovers and a refuge for many thousands of **migrating songbirds** that pass through Morocco each spring and autumn. The forest is threatened by overgrazing from cattle, goats and sheep, but is still home to many rare bird species, including the black-shouldered kite. Its **temporary lakes**, which appear during and after winter rains, attract waders and water-fowl, including storks. Migrant species include spotted flycatcher, roller and turtle dove.

CASABLANCA

Casablanca is Morocco's largest and most modern city, with a population exceeding three million people and the largest share of the country's industry and inter-national trade, including more than half of its shipping. Casablanca is Africa's fourth busiest port in terms of shipping, but unlike most of the world's great mercantile centres, it has no natural harbour. Instead, the 3180m (3500yd) Moulay Youssef Jetty shelters ships from the Atlantic breakers. This is a cosmopolitan city, more Europeanized than any other in Morocco and perhaps in the whole Arab world. The **new town** surrounds – and is very much larger than – the

Below: *The elaborately arched interior of the grandiose Mosque of Hassan II, Casablanca's most important landmark.*

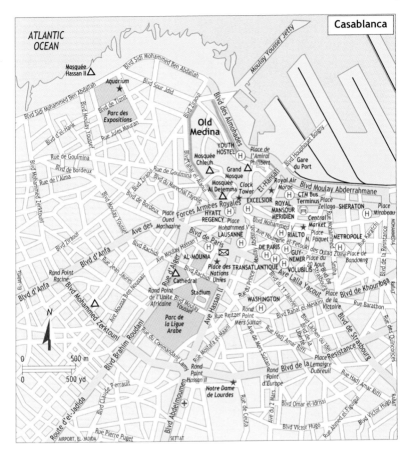

older **medina** and is a hectic metropolis with undistinguished high-rise office and apartment blocks
overshadowing older and shabbier buildings dating from
the 1930s. Towering over the entire urban landscape is
the magnificent **Hassan II Mosque** (one of the largest
religious buildings in the Islamic world), which was
conceived by the late king in the finest traditions of his
predecessors. The mosque is one of the very few religious
buildings in Morocco that can be visited by non-Muslims,
and should not be missed. There is not much history here,

Above: *This fountain in the Hassan II Mosque is decorated with brilliantly patterned tilework.*

and even less of the romantic and somewhat sinister atmosphere of the Casablanca that existed between the two world wars and during World War II, when the city was a byword for intrigue and espionage.

Hassan II Mosque ★★★

No expense was spared in the building of the colossal mosque, with its 200m (650ft) **minaret** (the world's tallest). The prayer hall can accommodate 25,000 people, with space for 80,000 on the esplanade outside. More than 3000 craftsmen were employed on its 67,000m² (720,000 sq ft) of plaster, 10,000m² (108,000 sq ft) of tile and paintwork, and 53,000m² (570,000sq ft) of carved and panelled wood. The whole project cost some US$800 million. Unlike almost all other Muslim religious buildings in Morocco, the mosque is open to non-Muslims (on guided tours only, Saturday–Thursday four times daily at 09:00, 10:00, 11:00 and 14:00).

The Medina ★

Southwest of the port, entered via Place de l'Amiral Philibert, Casablanca's medina area is unexciting but not unattractive, with a mix of everyday **shops** and **workshops** as well as **souvenir stalls** aimed at tourists.

AZEMMOUR

About 85km (53 miles) south of Casablanca, Azemmour was briefly (1513–41) occupied by the Portuguese who built an outpost surrounded by ochre-coloured battlements overlooking the Oum er-Rbia river. It is not much visited, but the **medina**, with its blindingly white, cubic houses and splashes of bougainvillea, is very attractive and there is a good **Atlantic beach** at **Haouiza** around 2km (1 mile) from the town centre.

EL-JADIDA

El-Jadida, 100km (62 miles) south of Casablanca, has the best anchorage on Morocco's entire Atlantic coast and so was **strategically important** to the Portuguese, who hung on here until 1769 when they were driven out by Sidi Mohammed bin Abdallah. The Portuguese blew up their **fortress** before they left, and the **ramparts** were not rebuilt until the 1820s. The square **Cité Portugaise** (Portuguese City), with a formidable bastion at each corner, commands the harbour, with water on two sides, and is surrounded by the modern part of town. Sadly, El-Jadida's beaches, which extend both sides of town, are dirty, and crowded in summer.

Cité Portugaise ★★★

The entrance to the old Portuguese fortified city is off Place Mohammed bin Abdallah, at the north end of Boulevard de Suez. The **ramparts** can be reached either through the entrance next to the southwest bastion, or from the harbour at the east end of Rue Mohammed Ahchemi.

Citerne Portugaise ★★★

The most spectacular aspect of the quarter is the **Portuguese Cistern**, which is situated midway along Rue Mohammed Ahchemi, the main street through the Portuguese City. Within the enormous 1100m² (12,000 sq ft) chamber, stone pillars support a massively vaulted roof. This was the city's **water supply**, enabling it to hold out against long sieges. It is open 08:30–12:00 and 14:30–18:00 daily.

> ### TOP HOLE
>
> The **Royal Golf Dar es Salam** is Morocco's top golf course. Designed by Robert Trent-Jones, the 45-hole course attracts leading professional golfers for the Hassan II Tournament in November each year and is regarded as one of the most formidable in the world. It is also one of the most beautiful courses, lushly landscaped with flowering trees. Its water hazards attract colourful wild birds, including flamingoes.

Below: *Formidable bastions built by the Portuguese command the harbour at El-Jadida.*

Rabat, Casablanca and Surrounds at a Glance

BEST TIMES TO VISIT

Rabat and Casablanca can be visited year-round, but the Atlantic Coast is sunniest Jun–Sep and can be cool and wet Jan–Mar. Best times: Apr–Sep. Rain is possible Dec–Apr; coastal fog even in summer.

GETTING THERE

By Air: British Airways (www.ba.com) from London Gatwick and EasyJet (www.easyjet.com) from London Luton several times weekly. **By Rail:** Trains to Rabat and Casablanca from Tangier, Fez, Meknès, Marrakech and other towns. **By Road:** Long-distance buses go between Rabat and Casablanca and connect them with all other large towns and cities. Long-distance taxis (*grands taxis*) run between Casablanca and Rabat, Casablanca and Essaouira, and Rabat and Fez.

GETTING AROUND

As in other Moroccan cities, **taxis** are cheap and the most convenient way of getting around Casablanca and Rabat. City **buses** not recommended.

WHERE TO STAY

Rabat

LUXURY

Villa Mandarine, 19 rue Ouled Bousbaa, tel: (037) 75 20 77, www.villamandarine.com Five km (3 miles) from the city centre, this is Rabat's most sybaritic address, set in its own gardens with pretty rooms and excellent facilities.

MID-RANGE

Mercure Hotel Sheherazade, 21 rue de Tunis, Quartier Hassan, tel: (037) 72 22 26, www.mercure.com Comfortable modern hotel, very affordable rate for a three-star.

BUDGET

Hotel Splendid, 8 rue Ghazza, tel/fax: (037) 72 32 83. Large, clean rooms, some with en-suite shower and WC, in a 1930s colonial building.

Casablanca

LUXURY

Royal Mansour Meridien, 27 Avenue des FAR, tel: (022) 31 30 11, www.starwoodhotels.com Deluxe five-star, elegant hotel with large luxury rooms, excellent service, fine food and evening entertainment.

MID-RANGE

Hotel Transatlantique, 79 rue Chaouia, tel: (022) 29 45 51, www.transatcasa.com Great value for money, with its 1920s surroundings, two bars and comfortable rooms.

BUDGET

Hotel Casablanca, 83 rue de la Liberte, tel: (022) 44 02 02, fax: (022) 31 84 04. Rooms have en-suite bathrooms, TV and direct-dial telephones. Blandly decorated.

WHERE TO EAT

Rabat

Luxury

Dinarjat, 6 Rue Belgnaoui, tel: (037) 70 42 39. Moroccan gastronomy at its best, excellent food served in a lavish setting.

Le Goland, 9 Rue Moulay Ali Cherif, tel: (037) 76 88 85. Superb Moroccan and international menu; best known for its delicious seafood.

Grill Kanoun, 2 Rue d'Ifni (Hôtel Rabat Chellah), tel: (037) 70 10 51. One of Rabat's better hotel restaurants, specializing in meat dishes grilled over wood fires.

MID-RANGE

Au Crepuscule, Rue Mohamed El Jazouli, tel: (037) 72 17 13. Good grilled meat dishes, a superb seafood platter as speciality.

Le Grand Comptoir, 279 ave Mohamed V, tel: (037) 20 15 14. One of Rabat's fashionable new eating and meeting places, in a restored 1930s grand café. Great atmosphere.

La Mamma (closed Sundays), 6 Zankat Tanta, tel: (037) 70 73 29. Popular pizzeria.

BUDGET

Restaurant-Pub Le Puzzle, 79 Avenue Ibn Sina, tel: (037) 67 00 30. Restaurant-bar serving Moroccan and international dishes, with live jazz.

Casablanca

LUXURY

Riad Zitoun, 31 Bd Rachidi,

tel: (022) 22 39 27. Fine Moroccan dishes such as pigeon couscous, on an open air terrace in summer.

Al Mounia, 95 rue du Prince Moulay Abdullah, tel: (022) 22 26 69. Arrive early or book for an outdoor table at this popular restaurant with a good Moroccan menu.

MID-RANGE

Le Petit Poucet, 86 Bd Mohammed V, tel: (022) 27 54 20. Pleasantly old-fashioned, French-style, good seafood.

La Broche, 123 rue el Arrar, tel: (022) 27 85 99. Pleasant restaurant, international menu (emphasizing French Provençal cooking) at competitive prices.

BUDGET

La Sqala, Ave. des Almohades, tel: (022) 26 09 60. Modern Asian-Moroccan meals and snacks in a pretty garden terrace or indoors in 'café Maure' ambience.

La Taverne du Dauphin, 115 Boulevard Houphouet Boigny, tel: (022) 22 12 00. Excellent fish restaurant with bar, also serves snacks and light meals.

TOURS AND EXCURSIONS

Tours by coach and/or air to Fez, Marrakech, Meknès, the Atlas and the desert valleys and oases are operated by numerous agencies in Rabat and Casablanca and can be booked through major hotels or through travel agencies.

Sud Voyages, Boulevard de la

Corniche, Ain Daib, Casablanca, tel: (022) 39 17 59, fax: (022) 39 54 22. Desert and Atlas mountain tours, trips to the other imperial cities, and game fishing cruises.

Pottery

A taxi will take you to the potters' village, 2km (1.5 miles) outside the city on the main road to Meknès, where you can watch potters making earthenware *tajines*, pots and jars, and buy decorated pottery gifts.

Sport

Golf

Rabat has a good golf course, the **Royal Golf Dar es Salam**, 10km (6 miles) out of town on Route de Zaers, tel: (037) 75 58 64, fax: (037) 75 76 71.

USEFUL CONTACTS

Rabat

Regional Tourist Office, 22 Avenue d'Alger, tel: (037) 73 05 62, fax: (037) 72 79 17.

Moroccan National Tourist Office (MNTO), corner rue Oued and rue Zellaga, tel: (037) 67 39 18.

CTM Bus Terminus, Route de Casablanca,

tel: (037) 43 82 82.

Railway Station, Avenue Mohammed V, tel: (090) 20 30 40, www.oncf.ma

Casablanca

Regional Tourist Office, 98 Boulevard Mohammed V, tel: (022) 22 11 77.

MNTO, 55 Rue Omar Slaoui, tel: (022) 27 95 33.

CTM Bus Terminus, 23 Rue Leon l'Africain, tel: (022) 36 13 04/36 07 73.

Railway stations: Tel: (09) 20 30 40, www.oncf.ma Casablanca has two main rail stations. Trains for all destinations use **Casa-Voyageurs**, on Place de la Gare at the east end of Boulevard Mohamed V, tel: (022) 24 38 18, fax: (022) 24 08 08. **Gare du Port** (trains to Fez, Oujda, Rabat and Tangier) or **Casa-Port** station, entrance to the commercial port, cnr Boulevard Houphouet Boigny and Boulevard Moulay Abderrahmane, tel: (022) 27 18 37.

Royal Air Maroc, 44 Avenue des FAR, tel: (022) 31 11 22, fax: (022) 44 24 09.

Aeroport Mohammed V, Route de Marrakech, tel: (022) 53 90 40.

RABAT	J	F	M	A	M	J	J	A	S	O	N	D
AVERAGE TEMP. °F	64	66	68	72	75	77	79	79	77	75	68	61
AVERAGE TEMP. °C	18	19	20	22	24	25	26	26	25	24	20	16
HOURS OF SUN DAILY	6	7	8	9	11	12	12	12	12	12	8	7
RAINFALL in	2.5	2.5	2.5	2	1	0.2	0	0	0.3	1	2	2
RAINFALL mm	52	52	53	40	25	5	0	0	8	25	40	40
DAYS OF RAINFALL	15	15	20	10	8	1	0	0	2	10	10	12

5
Marrakech and Around

Probably the best known and most visited of Morocco's historic cities, **Marrakech** – 240km (150 miles) south of Casablanca – stands on plains, which not far away give way to the foothills of the High Atlas, with **Jebel Toubkal**, the highest summit in the Atlas ranges, only 56km (35 miles) to the southeast. The **Oued Tensift**, rising in the foothills of the Atlas, flows through the city on its way to the Atlantic. Marrakech is surrounded by palm gardens and fertile farmland watered by the Tensift and other streams flowing out of the Atlas.

Three very different towns on the Mediterranean coast – **Safi**, 270km (170 miles) south of Casablanca; **Essaouira**, 128km (80 miles) south of Safi; and **Agadir**, 172km (107 miles) south of Essaouira – are all within a few hours' drive of Marrakech and a visit to the city can be combined with a visit to any or all of these.

Safi is a modern fishing port and industrial centre surrounding a historic harbour and walled medina; Essaouira is a medieval fortress city with strong Portuguese influences; and Agadir, devastated by an earthquake during the 1960s, is a purpose-built tourism resort attracting a mainly mass-market northern European clientele.

MARRAKECH

Marrakech is one of the most magical of Morocco's cities. Once within the pink plastered walls of its old town – where the spires of minarets and the crests of palm trees rise above a labyrinth of narrow alleys, and

---

DON'T MISS

★★★ Djemaa el-Fna: Square of the Dead, the gateway to the bustling medina of Marrakech.
★★★ Essaouira: a coastal town with great beaches, a picturesque harbour and fine seafood.
★ Agadir: a purpose-built holiday resort with some excellent beaches.

Opposite: *In Marrakech, men dressed as traditional water sellers pose for a tourist's camera.*

CHERMOULA

Many dishes are accompanied by a dish of spicy chermoula, one of Morocco's favourite **condiments**. This pungent relish is a blend of fresh ginger and garlic, green chilli, shallots, onions, leeks, plenty of coriander, white pepper and cumin, and is a superb accompaniment to fish dishes. There is no fixed recipe, and the proportion of ingredients is to the maker's taste.

the serrated peaks of the High Atlas dominate the eastern horizon – the modern boulevards of the new town are quickly forgotten.

During the colonial era, the sultan's palace was converted into one of Morocco's grandest hotels, the **Mamounia**, whose guest list includes such illustrious names as General de Gaulle (who made it his headquarters after his Free French troops reclaimed Morocco from the Vichy government), Winston Churchill, Paul McCartney (who wrote a song about it) and painter David Hockney (who made several paintings of its fantastic pool with palm trees and islands). Later, the 1960s hippies rode the **Marrakech Express** to the town that had become one of the legends of the hippy trail.

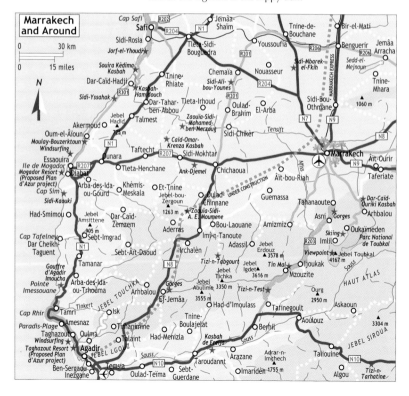

Marrakech and Around

Founded as long ago as the 11th century, Marrakech is a city rich in relics of an illustrious past, but with a living heritage that is equally vibrant. Its population of around 1.5 million people makes it Morocco's fourth largest city, and beyond a doubt it is – as it has been for almost 1000 years – the most important in southern Morocco.

Above: *A decorative window in Marrakech's Jardin Majorelle.*

Historically, Marrakech had close links with Morocco's deep south, and traded its goods for gold, slaves and ivory from the great African kingdoms south of the Sahara. Muslim missionaries carried the message of Islam down the great **caravan routes** from Marrakech into Africa, and for a while Marrakech was the hub of a vast sprawling empire that extended as far as modern-day Mali, Niger and Chad. Like all Moroccan cities, Marrakech is divided into an old walled **medina** and a **new town** built during the French occupation.

VILLE NOUVELLE

The hub of the new town is the Place du 16 Novembre, with the Avenue Mohammed V connecting it with the Place de la Liberté and running through the **Bab Larissa** (Larissa Gate) into the medina. The new town is uninspiring, but boasts two of the lovely **landscaped gardens** for which Marrakech is known.

Jardin Majorelle ★★

Off Avenue Yacoub al-Mansour, the flower-filled gardens were first designed and planted by **Jacques Majorelle**, an undistinguished French painter who lived in the blue-painted mansion in the centre of the gardens. The villa (now with a small Islamic art gallery) and gardens are owned by French couturier **Yves St Laurent**, but are open to visitors. Open 08:00–12:00 and 14:00–17:00 daily, (15:00–19:00 June–September).

> ### PALM GARDENS
>
> Morocco has almost five million **date palms**, and palm plantations cover at least 80,000ha (200,000 acres). There are more than 100 varieties of date. They can readily be dried and preserved and so have always been a valuable source of nutrition for the nomads and pastoralists of the desert and its borderlands. Oasis dwellers use every part of the tree, which can grow to more than 30m (100ft), but lives for less than 10 years. Leaf fronds are woven into baskets and mats, trunks are used in building houses. The wood and fronds are also used for kindling and firewood.

Above: *Overlooking the Djemaa el-Fna and the gateway to the medina is the elegant minaret of the Koutoubia Mosque.*

Jardin de la Menara ★

Situated well out of the city centre (about 3km/ 2 miles southwest on Avenue de la Menara), the Menara Garden was laid out as a summer retreat for the sultan and his ministers. Olive, palm and citrus groves surround a central pool. Open dawn to dusk daily.

THE MEDINA

In many Moroccan cities (such as Fez and Meknès), you plunge immediately into the narrow lanes of the souk as soon as you pass through the gates of the medina. In Marrakech, the labyrinthine inner souk, north of the Djemaa el-Fna, is surrounded by broader streets, gardens and avenues, overlooked by the minarets of many mosques and the turrets and crenellated walls of princely palaces, the lasting legacy of the succession of dynasties that made Marrakech their capital. Avenue Mohammed V enters the medina by the Bab Larissa. The landmark **Koutoubia Mosque** stands on the south side of the avenue, and from here the Rue el-Koutoubia leads north to the **Djemaa el-Fna**, the heart and soul of the medina and the best place to start exploring.

Djemaa el-Fna ★★★

The Djemaa el-Fna (Square of the Dead) is a wide plaza with the entrance to Morocco's labyrinth of souks, Rue Souq as-Smarrine, leading off its north side. Quiet until noon, the square rapidly fills up in the early afternoon, when it becomes the domain of juice sellers, peddlers, jugglers, acrobats, storytellers, snake-charmers, fire-eaters, magicians and fortune tellers. At sunset, these give way to dozens of food stalls.

Koutoubia Mosque ★★★

The 70m (230ft) minaret of the Koutoubia Mosque towers over the medina, a symbol of the city and of Morocco. Built in the late 12th century, it became a

---

BERBER ACROBATS

The Berber acrobats of southern Morocco have been famous for more than a century, and many of the best-known circuses in Europe feature troupes of Berber tumblers recruited in Morocco, often in Marrakech's Djemaa el-Fna. Their stunts may originally have been a form of military training, but today their extreme agility is used only in entertainment.

model for many others throughout the country. Much of its original decoration has recently been restored, but the mosque is not open to non-Muslims.

Ali ben Youssef Medersa ★★

The Ali ben Youssef Mosque, at the corner of Rue Souq as-Smarrine and Rue de Bab Debbagh (just north of the souk), is the **oldest mosque** in Marrakech and one of its largest. Built in the 12th century, it shows little trace of its age, having been entirely reconstructed during the 19th century. The mosque is not open to unbelievers, but you can usually visit the Ali ben Youssef Medersa next door. The *medersa* dates from 1565 but, like the mosque, has been extensively renovated. Inside, it is cool and tranquil, with fine examples of stucco, mosaic and carved woodwork. Austere students' cells on the second floor of the two-storey complex surround seven courtyards, the largest of which is overlooked by the mosque. Open from 09:00 until sunset, Sunday–Thursday.

MARRAKECH MOSQUES

A forest of minarets rises above the medina, but from outside, in the narrower streets, it is hard to get a good look at most of Marrakech's historic mosques, and their interiors are off-limits to non-Muslims. Among the most important are the **Ali ben Youssef Mosque** – built in the 12th century – and the **Mouassine Mosque**, dating from the 16th century. The green mosaic spire of the **Ben Salah Mosque**, built in 1321, is another eminent landmark.

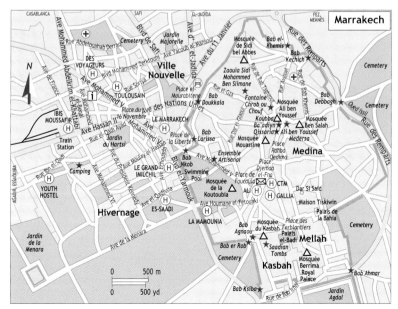

Koubba Ba'adiyn ★

The *koubba* (meeting hall) is a small **pavilion**, a rare survival from the Almoravid era in the 12th century and one of the few examples of Islamic architecture in Marrakech that can be entered by non-Muslims. Opposite the Ali ben Youssef Mosque, it is an attractive, well-proportioned little building. Open 09:00–17:00, Sunday–Thursday.

The Souks ★★★

Rue Souq as-Smarrine runs off the north side of Djemaa el-Fna and is the main thoroughfare through Marrakech's labyrinth of souks, with different areas devoted to crafts and products, including textiles, pottery, carpets, sheep-skins, carpentry and coppersmithing. You can **hire a guide** to steer you through the maze, but bear in mind that he will undoubtedly also steer you into shops that pay him commission on what you buy. It can be more enjoyable to wander at random through the souks: it is difficult to lose your way completely, and keeping to the larger thorough-fares will eventually lead you out of the labyrinth. The souks are definitely not to be missed.

At the southern end of Souq as-Smarrine, most shops cater to tourists in search of souvenirs, rugs, blankets,

and metalwork. Heading to the north, the souks become more authentic: you can detour into the *qissaria* (covered market), the carpet-weaver's area at **Place Rahba Qedima** (also called the Berber Souk), the dyers' souk (where the walls, pavement and workers are splashed and stained with crimson, orange and deep purple from the dye vats) and the woodworkers' and metal-smiths' souks.

THE KASBAH

Marrakech's kasbah lies in the southwest corner of the medina walls, surrounded by an inner rampart. Immediately east of the kasbah walls lies the former mellah (Jewish quarter), now almost entirely Muslim – although

its architecture is still distinctively different from the rest of the medina. A modern **Royal Palace** (closed to visitors) occupies the southeast sector of the old kasbah.

Palais el-Badi ★

The El-Badi or Badia Palace was built by **Ahmed al-Mansour**, one of Marrakech's greatest sultans, and completed in 1602. It was a lavish affair of marble, tile, stucco and rare woods but, in 1696, **Sultan Moulay Ismail** chose to recycle these materials to build his own new capital city at Meknès, and what you see today is no more than a quadrangle of crumbling ramparts surrounding an orange garden. Open daily 08:30–12:00 and 14:30–18:00.

Jardin Agdal ★

Another of Marrakech's extensive gardens, filled with palms, citrus and almond trees and flowering shrubs, the **Agdal Garden** occupies several square kilometres to the south of the Royal Palace. Access is sometimes restricted for royal security reasons; check with the tourist office before visiting.

Palais de la Bahia ★

Off Rue Riad Zitoun el-Jedidi, the relatively modern Bahia Palace was built in 1894 and later became the **official residence** of France's governor in Marrakech. The governor's elegant apartments and state rooms are in disrepair, but the gardens are an attractive place to relax for a while. Open 08:30–13:00 and 16:00–19:00 daily.

Above: *The famed Djemaa el-Fna (the Square of the Dead) is the hub of the Marrakech medina.*
Opposite: *Brilliantly glazed dishes, bowls and* tajine *cooking pots piled high in a Marrakech potter's shop.*

THE SQUARE OF THE DEAD

The origins of the Djemaa el-Fna's name are lost in the mists of time. Literally translated, it means 'gathering place of the dead' – a name which probably refers to the practice (which continued into the 19th century) of executing criminals and rebels here and displaying their heads in the market place.

Dar Si Said ★★★

In what was once the mansion of the Saadian prince **Sidi Said** (off Rue Riad Zitoun el-Jedidi, one block north of Bahia Palace), the collection of fine Moroccan crafts from jewellery to pottery, leatherwork and silversmithing in the **Museum of Moroccan Art** is dazzling – with surroundings to match. The house is superbly decorated. Open Wednesday–Monday, 09:00–18:00.

Maison Tiskiwin ★★★

This **private museum** in the home of Dutch expat **Bert Flint**, next to Bahia Palace, is a treasure house of **Berber craftsmanship**. Flint has lived in Morocco since 1950 and has gathered a magnificent collection of textiles, jewellery, leatherwork and carved wooden doors from Berber kasbahs. Open daily 09:00–18:00.

Above: *The superb geometric decorative work in the Saadian tombs is among the finest examples of Moorish craftsmanship.*

Saadian Tombs ★★

In the northwest corner of the kasbah, south of the **Kasbah Mosque** (which is closed to non-Muslims), this complex of mausoleums dates from the Saadian dynasty of the late 16th century. Sultan **Ahmed al-Mansour**, who also ordered the building of the El-Badi palace, was the first to be buried here and more than 60 of his successors and their families were eventually interred in these elaborate coffers. **Moulay Ismail**, the second sultan (1672–1727) of the Alaouite dynasty, had the tombs sealed and they were almost forgotten until as late as 1917 when they were reopened by the French resident-general, General Lyautey. They are among the best surviving examples of the skill of Moorish craftsmen from Al-Andalus. Open daily (except Friday mornings) 08:00–12:00 and 14:30–19:00.

SAFI

Safi is, at first sight, not the most charming of Morocco's coastal towns, surrounded as it is by canning factories and phosphate processing plants. Nevertheless, this important **sardine fishing port** has an attractive old **medina**, within walls that shut it off from the banal modern town. Like Essaouira, its good natural harbour attracted the Portuguese, who seized the town in 1508 and built a small fortress whose battlements still guard the old port. The Portuguese were ejected in 1541, and today Safi's medina is dwarfed by the modern city that surrounds it but is worth exploring: it is entered via Rue du Souq, which runs from Rue du Rabat (the main coastal highway) eastward through the medina to the Bab Chaba gate on its east side.

Qasr al-Bahr ★★

This small Portuguese fortress (its Arabic name means 'castle on the sea') is now the residence of the city governor. Rebuilt in 1963, its battlements still have their **cannon** and you can ascend the dungeon tower for a panoramic view of the medina, coast and harbour. It is open 08:30–12:00 and 14:30–18:00 daily.

The Medina ★★

Rue du Souq, running through the medina, meets Rue du Rabat just across the road from Qasr al-Bahr. Safi's medina is less

---

GNAOUA BROTHERHOOD

Most numerous in the south, the Gnaoua fraternity is part of a broader movement of **Sufi** mystics, dancers and musicians whose musical ceremonies are claimed to heal the sick and those believed to be possessed by demons. Their music shows strong **African influences**, and their instruments – including the stringed *sentri* – are very similar to those used in Mali, Niger and Chad.

Below: *On many Moroccan quaysides you can choose your fresh seafood and have it cooked to your taste.*

COASTAL CITADELS

The Portuguese and Spanish **fortresses** dotted down the coast from Asilah to Essaouira and points south will look oddly familiar to anyone who has visited Mombasa, Goa or Macau. In the late 15th and early 16th centuries, Portuguese navigators such as Vasco da Gama and Fernando Poo sailed south down the coast of Africa, then across the Indian Ocean to India and the South China Sea. The forts along the Moroccan coast were the first links in a world-spanning chain of similar strongholds built to protect the harbours they seized for their empire.

tourist oriented than most, and there are fewer hustlers and less aggressive selling by shopkeepers, making it an interesting place in which to wander. Best of all is the **pottery souk**, just inside the walls before you reach Bab Chaba. It's a good place to buy pretty *tajine* vessels, bowls and plates to take home.

Musée National de Céramique (Kechla) ★★

Safi is known for producing some of the best colourfully glazed and elaborately patterned earthenware in Morocco. You can see fine examples of local work, as well as pottery from other parts of Morocco, in the **National Museum of Ceramics**, housed in the Kechla, the former arsenal at the eastern end of the roughly rectangular medina. It is open 09:00–12:00 and 14:30–18:00, Sunday–Thursday.

ESSAOUIRA

Essaouira, some 128km (80 miles) south of Safi, is a delightful small **harbour town** with a fine Portuguese **fortress**, a colourful walled **medina**, a port full of sardine fishing boats, a superb beach pounded by Atlantic surf and some excellent, very stylish places to stay. Recently discovered by trendy Europeans, it still has plenty of its original Moroccan character.

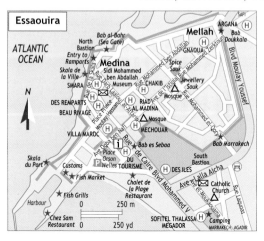

Known to the Portuguese as **Mogador**, Essaouira was one of the Maghreb's gateways to the European world as early as the first centuries BC, when the purple dye obtained from the murex (a type of shellfish), which thrived off the **Iles Purpuraires** (or Purple Islands), became a popular Roman commodity. During the 16th century, Mogador became one of Portugal's

most important posses-
sions along the Atlantic
coast and, after the
expulsion of the
Portuguese, it became
a vital trading port,
exchanging the gold
and ivory brought by
trans-Sahara camel car-
avans for European-
manufactured goods.

The town owes its
unique architectural
character to **Sultan Sidi
Mohammed ben Abdallah**, who, in 1765, imported
French architect **Théodore Cornut** to design a town that
would attract European merchants away from the rival
port of Agadir, which was then in the hands of rebels
against the Sultan.

Above: *Essaouira's
harbour is ringed by
battlements and crowded
with fishing boats large
and small.*

The Medina ★★
Cornut's **Porte de la Marine** (Sea Gate), leading through
a ring of ramparts into the medina, is still the town's
finest landmark, while the medina, instead of being a
typically Moroccan maze of alleys, is instead a grid of
relatively wide streets.

The Harbour Area ★★
Essaouira's attractive harbour is on a promontory point-
ing southwest into the Atlantic and guarded by the
ramparts of the **Skala du Port**. South of here, a wide,
sandy **beach** backed by tall sand dunes, stretches for
more than 10km (6 miles) south to Cap Sim. Atlantic
winds make it a world-class **windsurfing** spot.

When the sardine boats are offloading their silvery
catch, the harbour and its quayside fish market are a
colourful sight, if a bit smelly. You can eat deliciously
fresh sardines, straight off the boat and grilled in front
of you over a charcoal brazier, at the outdoor fish stalls
on the south side of the harbour.

A VARIETY OF SPICE

No Moroccan market is
complete without its spice
merchants, seated behind
long trestle tables covered
with conical heaps of
brilliantly coloured powders.
The aroma alone is
deliciously overpowering.
Cheaper spices are sold loose
by the kilogram but **saffron**,
the most precious, is sold by
the gram in tiny paper sachets.
True saffron is the bright
yellow pollen of a species of
crocus; unscrupulous traders
may try to pass off the much
cheaper, equally vivid
turmeric, as the real thing.

Skala du Port ★★

Situated on the northern side of the harbour, facing the Atlantic, the Skala du Port (Harbour Fort) – a fortress founded by the Portuguese and embellished by Cornut – offers visitors postcard views of the harbour and also great Atlantic sunsets.

Skala de la Ville ★★★

The Skala de la Ville (City Fortress) is about 400m (1300ft) north of the port, facing the Atlantic and just outside the city walls. It still has its formidable collection of **18th-century brass cannons**, imported from Europe by the modernizing Sidi Mohammed ben Abdallah. Like its sister-fortress, it has fine sea views and also offers an excellent panorama of the medina.

Above: *The imposing battlements of the Skala du Port dominate the old fishing harbour at Essaouira.*

The Medina ★★★

Enter Essaouira's unique and charmingly laid-back medina from the harbour via Place Prince Moulay Hassan or through the **Bab al-Bahr** (Sea Gate) 200m (650ft) off the Skala de la Ville. Place Prince Moulay Hassan leads onto Rue Mohammed ben Abdallah, one of the main streets through the medina. The other main thoroughfare is Avenue Oqba ben Nafi/Avenue de l'Istiqlal/Rue Zerktouni, which exits the medina walls via the northern **Bab Doukkala** (Doukkala Gate). Two fascinating souks, the **Jewellery Souk** and the **Spice Souk**, flank each side of Avenue de l'Istiqlal, just beyond its junction with Rue Mohammed el-Qory.

Sidi Mohammed ben Abdallah Museum ★★

The former pasha's (governor's) residence, on Rue Darb Laalouj al-Attarin (north of Place Prince Moulay Hassan), is a fine example of a **decorated Moroccan façade**, and houses a wealth of art treasures from Essaouira and the surrounding region, including weapons, textiles, ceramics and jewellery. Open daily, 09:00–18:00.

The Islands ★

Now uninhabited, the **Ile de Mogador** (within sight of the harbour to the southwest) was another Portuguese garrison and one of the keys to controlling the coast. Its substantial fortress became a prison under the French. Next to the fortress island is another medium-sized island, while around it are the **Iles Purpuraires**, or Purple Islands. The murex (*see* page 100) that flourished around their shores were the much-prized source of purple dye, so highly valued by Romans and Byzantines that only the Emperor was permitted to wear purple.

The islands are also one of the few breeding places of the endangered **Eleanora's falcon**, which migrates all the way from Madagascar to breed here in summer. When the falcons are in residence the islands are off-limits to visitors, but for the rest of the year boat trips and scuba diving can be arranged through the Essaouira tourist office.

Left: *Colourful spices and herbs piled on display in the market at Essaouira.*

BRINGING THEM BACK

Efforts are being made to restore some of Morocco's vanished or **endangered species** by reintroducing breeding pairs of animals from breeding zoos and reserves in other countries. **Oryx** have been reintroduced into the **Parc National de Souss Massa** in a joint effort with several European zoos, and **addax** (a species of antelope) have also been reintroduced in the Souss. Other species include **Barbary deer**, **partridge** and **pheasant** species, and the **Mediterranean monk seal**.

AGADIR

Agadir, 172km (107 miles) south of Essaouira, is the most tourist-oriented town in Morocco, having been purpose built as a **tourist resort** for middle-income European visitors. In 1960, the city was levelled by an earthquake, with the loss of some 15,000 lives as well as all of its historic buildings. The decision was taken to rebuild the city with package tourism in mind and with its excellent **sandy beach** as its main attraction. The result is not very different from any other mass-market resort on the Mediterranean, although it retains a Moroccan flavour. At least Agadir has not gone the high-rise hotel route, with most of its three- and four-star resorts more or less concealed by palms and bougainvillea.

The beach, sheltered by a headland jutting into the Atlantic, is much less windswept than the beach at Essaouira, and its long summers and mild winters make it a year-round favourite – people from Scandinavia, the Netherlands and Germany even drive their motor homes all the way to Agadir to escape the northern winter.

Agadir also has its merits as a base for exploring the **High Atlas** and the **Anti Atlas**, or heading on down south

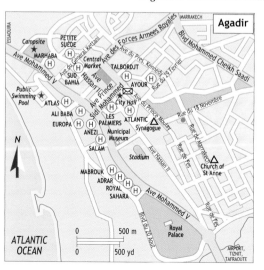

along the increasingly deserted Atlantic coast or into the Western Sahara. It is also an important **fishing port**, although the modern trawler harbour is well to the north of the main resort area. Agadir's best hotels are located along the ocean-front, with the cheaper properties inland. Agadir is laid out on a grid plan, and has a range of amenities, including a modern sports stadium and a public swimming pool, but for sightseeing it cannot really compete with most other Moroccan cities – even its walled kasbah fell victim to the 1960 earthquake. To compensate, it has probably the best variety of **water sports** and activities in Morocco, and a good range of excursion companies offering a number of tours around central and southern Morocco.

Kasbah ★

About 2km (1 mile) north (follow Rue de la Corniche out of town), on a hill overlooking the trawler harbour, the old kasbah is all that remains of the original Agadir, which surrounded it. Now all that remains of the old medina is the grassy mound called the **Ancienne Talborjt**, where most of those killed in the earthquake were buried in a mass grave. To make sure the tragedy of 1960 is not repeated, the new Agadir has been designed to be earthquake-proof. Of the kasbah itself, only the partly rebuilt outer walls remain.

Musée du Patrimoine Amazigh ★

Opened in 2000, the Amazigh Heritage Museum has a superb collection of traditional jewellery from the villages of the region – more than 900 items in all. Open 09:30–13:00 and 14:30–18:00 Monday–Saturday.

Musée des Arts Populaires ★

This small museum boasts a good collection of Berber and Saharan textiles and leatherwork donated by Bert Flint, owner of Maison Tiskiwin in Marrakech (see page 98). Open 09:30–13:00 and 14:30–18:00 Monday–Saturday.

Souss Estuary ★

The river Souss, rising in the High Atlas close to Taroudannt, 80km (50 miles) inland, flows into the Atlantic 3km (2 miles) south of Agadir (just north of Inezgane). The mouth of the river and the beaches to either side are a haven for **waterfowl** – flamingoes and spoonbill are among the more spectacular species, but this is also a likely stop for a wide range of endemic and migrant wildfowl, waders, terns and gulls.

Above: *Sun loungers and umbrellas line the sweeping Atlantic beach at Agadir.*

FANTASIA

A full-scale *fantaisie*, or fantasia, can be a dramatic sight, with Berber horsemen, armed and cloaked, riding their horses at full gallop while firing their *moukhala* (muzzle-loading muskets) into the air. The fantasia dates from the early 19th century, when warrior clans sought to impress chiefs and sultans with their warlike skills. When Moroccan troops were brought into the French army, it became a more formal military affair. The fantasias advertised by some Agadir hotels are pathetic affairs, with no more than a dozen riders in unconvincing costume cantering past on tired-looking nags.

Marrakech and Around at a Glance

Marrakech can be extremely hot in summer, and cool and wet in winter. Apr–Jun and Oct–Dec are best. The Atlantic coast is cooler and wetter Dec–Apr and coastal fog possible even in summer. Best times are Apr–Oct.

By Air: Direct flights by Royal Air Maroc from Europe (Paris, London, Rome), connecting flights to Casablanca. There are connecting flights between Agadir and Casablanca and direct charter flights to Agadir from many European cities. EasyJet (www.easyjet.com) and British Airways (www.ba.com) from London Gatwick.
By Rail: The legendary, overnight Marrakech Express leaves Casablanca at midnight and arrives in Marrakech around 06:30. There are rail connections to other cities via Casablanca.
By Road: CTM and other buses connect Marrakech with Agadir, Essaouira, Casablanca, Fez, Ouarzazate and other major cities. CTM buses also operate on the coastal route between Agadir and Casablanca and from Essaouira to Casablanca. Long-haul taxis also operate.

Taxis are cheap and the most convenient way to go between the new town and the medina. In the medina, **horse-drawn** carriages can be hired by the hour or day. Inside the souk, **walking** is the only option.

Marrakech
LUXURY
Les Borjs de la Kasbah, tel: (242) 24 38 11 01, www. lesborjsdelakasbah.com Marrakech's newest and greenest hotel de charme has a spa and pool, gets its electricity from solar power, and has a super restaurant. Eighteen rooms, prices start at 12 dirhams per double per night.
Kasbah Agafay, Route de l'Aeroport, tel: (044) 42 09 60, fax: (044) 42 09 70. Magnificent (and expensive) hotel in a restored Berber fort on a hilltop 20km (12 miles) from the city centre; 13 suites, terraced gardens, pool and *hammam*.

MID-RANGE
Hôtel Mansour Eddahbi, Avenue de France, tel: (044) 44 82 22, fax: (044) 44 90 78. In new town, but only 500m (550yd) from the medina, huge (441 rooms) comfortable hotel with lush grounds, a lavish pool and fine restaurants.
Hôtel Myriem, 154 Avenue Mohammed el-Beqal, tel: (044) 43 70 62, fax: (044) 43 70 66. Modern hotel with pool in centre of the new town.

Essaouira
LUXURY
Ryad Mogador, Route de Marrakech, BP 368, tel: (044) 78 35 55, fax: (044) 78 35 56. Resort hotel, good location.

MID-RANGE
Villa Maroc, 10 Rue Abdellah Ben Yassin, tel: (044) 47 61 47, fax: (044) 47 58 06. www. villa-maroc.com Charming, small hotel, blue and white decor, rooftop terrace, views over the medina to the ocean.

BUDGET
The Teahouse, 74 Rue Darb Laalouj, tel: (044) 78 35 43. English-owned riad with two apartments on the edge of the former Jewish quarter.

Agadir
LUXURY
Le Tikida Beach, Chemin des Dunes, tel: (044) 84 54 00, fax: (044) 84 58 62. Five-star resort away from centre, near Souss estuary, virtually private beach.

MID-RANGE
Hôtel Marhaba, Avenue Mohammed V, BP 346, tel: (044) 84 06 70, fax: (044) 84 35 29. Fine four-star hotel with pool, sea views, attractive gardens. All rooms have balconies.

BUDGET
Hôtel Petite Suède, corner Avenue du Général Kettani and Avenue Hassan II, tel: (044) 84 07 79, fax: (044) 84 00 57. Small, affordable, central. No pool. Some rooms have sea view.

Marrakech and Around at a Glance

Marrakech

LUXURY

Dar Moha, 81 rue Dar el
Bacha, tel: (044) 38 64 00,
www.darmoha.ma
Marrakech's best restaurant;
Moroccan cuisine with a modern twist in the walled garden
of the a 19th-century mansion.
Poolside tables, belly dancers
and traditional *gnaoua* musicians. Evenings only.
Le Yacout, 79 Sidi Ahmed
Soussi, Bab Doukkala, tel:
(044) 38 27 29. Medina fabu-
lous – dine beside a glowing
blue outdoor pool, beneath the
painted arches of an upstairs
salon, or lounge on cushions
in the main dining area while
listening to *gnaoua* musicians.
Jana and **Crystal**, Pacha
Marrakech, Avenue
Mohammed V, Zone Hoteliere
d l'Aguedal, tel: (044) 38 84
82/(044) 38 84 80. Twin
restaurants within Marrakech's
coolest club. Jana serves
Moroccan dishes. Crystal has
a colonial Art Deco look and
Mediterranean nouvelle menu.
Le Comptoir, Avenue
Echouada, tel: (044) 43 77 02.
Grills, salads, sticky pastries
and belly dancers in an array
of Berber tents.
Le Marocain, Hotel La
Mamounia, Ave Bab Jdid, tel:
(044) 38 86 00. Old-style
decadence in the medina's
oldest and grandest hotel.
Food is above average (like
the prices) but it's the atmosphere that counts.

MID-RANGE

Le Fondouk, 55 Souk al Fassi
Kaat Bennahid, tel: (044) 37
81 90. The most sophisticated
restaurant in the old town
combines Asian, French and
Moroccan influences.

BUDGET

Dar Zellij, 1 Kaasour
Sidi Benslimane, tel:
(044) 38 84 82. *Tajine*,
couscous and pastille in
a beautifully preserved medina mansion with painted
ceilings and walls covered in
colourful patterned tiles.
One of Marrakech's longest
established eating places –
the menu is good but traditional. From £10. Open
daily.
Café Arabe, 184 rue
Mouassine, tel: (044) 42
97 28. Italian-owned café-
restaurant with tables in the
courtyard of an old house in
the medina, on a rooftop terrace with great sunset views.
Chez Chegrouni, Djemaa el-
Fna, tel: (044) 43 41 32.
Friendly spot serving traditional *tajines*, pasta and other
favourites at ridiculously low
prices.

Marrakech
Regional Tourist Office,
Abdelmoumen Ben Ali
Square, tel: (044) 43 62 39/43
61 31, fax: (044) 43 60 57.
Tourist Information Bureau,
170 Mohammed V, tel: (044)
43 08 86, fax: (044) 43 60 57.
Marrakech Airport, tel: (044)
44 78 65, fax: (044) 44 92 19.

Essaouira
Regional Tourist Office,
54 Avenue Lalla Amina, tel:
(044) 78 35 32.
Tourist Information, 10 Rue
de Caire, tel: (044) 78 35 32,
www.essaouira.com

Agadir
Regional Tourist Office, Av
Mohammed VI, tel: (044) 84
63 77, fax: (044) 84 63 78.
Airport Tourist Office, Agadir
Al Massira Airport,
tel: (044) 83 90 77.
Tourist Information Office,
Avenue Mohammed V,
tel: (044) 84 03 07.

Safi
Regional Tourist Office, Rue
Imam Malek, tel: (044) 46 45
53, fax: (044) 62 45 53.

MARRAKECH	J	F	M	A	M	J	J	A	S	O	N	D
AVERAGE TEMP. °F	64	66	68	72	77	78	95	95	88	77	70	61
AVERAGE TEMP. °C	18	19	20	22	25	31	35	35	31	25	21	16
HOURS OF SUN DAILY	8	8	9	10	11	11	12	12	12	12	12	8
RAINFALL in	1	1	1	1	0.6	0.2	0	0	0.2	1	1	1
RAINFALL mm	25	26	27	27	15	5	2	2	5	25	26	26
DAYS OF RAINFALL	10	10	10	8	7	2	1	1	3	8	9	9

6. The High Atlas, Anti Atlas and Sahara

The Atlas mountains and desert fringes offer the most **dramatic scenery** in Morocco, together with fascinating glimpses of ways of life in mountain and desert villages that have changed little in centuries and are only now yielding to the 21st century. The sierra of the **High Atlas** sweeps in a crescent from the Atlantic coast inland of Agadir, northward to the **Middle Atlas**. At first clad in cedars and pines, the Atlas slopes rise to bare rocky peaks that glow red in the summer sun and in winter are capped by snow. The highest peak in North Africa, **Jebel Toubkal** is clearly visible from Marrakech, more than 60km (40 miles) away, and is flanked by almost equally dramatic summits. Even in high summer, these mountain slopes and valleys can offer some respite from the heat of the plains.

The **Berber villages** of the Atlas are characteristically clutters of box-like, flat-roofed, mud-brick houses, surrounded by green cultivated terraces that stand out vividly against bare hillsides. The highest villages are at some 2000m (6500ft) above sea level, and in spring villagers drive their flocks higher into the mountains to take advantage of seasonal pastures.

To the south of the High Atlas, and parallel to it, is the **Anti Atlas**, a sierra of lower peaks located between the High Atlas and the desert. Guelmin (or Goulimime), at the southern extremity of the Anti Atlas, is the gateway to the **desert south**, a vast area of flat, gravel and sand desert for almost 1500km (930 miles) to Morocco's southern border.

DON'T MISS

★★★ **Jebel Toubkal National Park:** the 4167m (13,670ft) summit of the peak in the centre of the park is the highest in Morocco.
★★★ **Drâa Valley:** a region of contrasting desert and oasis landscapes.
★★★ **Dadès Valley:** the valley of a thousand kasbahs.
★★★ **Todra Gorge:** Morocco's answer to the Grand Canyon.

Opposite: *The Drâa Valley, a lush green ribbon of fields and palmeries, contrasts sharply with the arid mountains and desert hills which surround it.*

Above: *The impressive walls of the Kasbah Taourirt, Ouarzazate.*

JEBEL TOUBKAL AND SURROUNDS

Jebel Toubkal ★★★

The 4167m (13,670ft) high summit of Jebel Toubkal dominates the Atlas for tens of kilometres around and is at the centre of the **Jebel Toubkal National Park**, which covers some 36,000ha (90,000 acres) of forest and mountainside. The mountain and the surrounding park offer some superb **trekking**, with treks to the summit of Toubkal taking two to three days from Imlil village, located 17km (11 miles) south of Asni and 55km (35 miles) south of Marrakech.

Tizi-n-Tichka ★★

Morocco's **highest vehicular pass**, the Tizi-n-Tichka, carries the main road that leads through the mountains to Ouarzazate and the desert fringes, at a height of approximately 2260m (7415ft).

TELOUET

A 31km (20-mile) detour off the main N9 highway, east of the Tizi-n-Tichka, brings you to the partly ruined village of Telouet, once the seat of the most powerful clan of the High Atlas, the **Glaoui chieftains**. The Glaoui controlled the only **caravan route** between Marrakech and Ouarzazate and held great influence in the High Atlas. Virtually independent of the Alaouite sultans, the Glaoui collaborated with the French, who made the last of the line, **Thami el-Glaoui**, pasha of Marrakech. With a taste for the high life that ran to champagne and Rolls Royces, he was deposed and his property confiscated after independence in 1956 by Mohammed V, who saw the Glaoui as possible rivals.

Dar Glaoui ★★★

The great **kasbah** of the Glaoui, backed by bare peaks and surrounded by pastures and terraced fields, stands on the banks of the Oued Imare in the centre of the village. Now dilapidated, its surviving **grand halls** – with their painted ceilings, finely coloured tiles and carved woodwork – are a reminder of the power of the Glaoui dynasty. Open 09:00–12:00 and 14:30–17:00 daily.

OUARZAZATE

Ouarzazate, 204km (129 miles) southeast of Marrakech on the N9 highway – a spectacular drive through the High Atlas – is the main starting point for tours of the

BERBER JEWELLERY

Tiznit (*see* page 117) is a centre of fine Berber **silver-smithing** and some of the finest silver work in Morocco originates here. Tourists from Agadir have pushed prices up, but you can still haggle for beautiful silver bracelets, anklets, brooches and tribal talisman necklaces hung with amber, coral, and semiprecious stones.

The High Atlas, Anti Atlas and Sahara

THE GLAOUIS

The Glaoui clan of Berber chieftains held sway over much of the Atlas region for more than two centuries before reaching the peak of their power as French puppets during the 1930s, when – after the defeat of the Berber rising of 1934 – the French installed **Mohammed el-Glaoui** as pasha (governor) of Marrakech. El-Glaoui took the opportunity to enrich himself and his clan, acquiring – among other Western playthings – a fleet of Rolls Royces. He died in 1957, shortly after independence.

south's most spectacular desert valleys, those of the **Drâa** and **Dadès** rivers. Built by the French in the 1920s, Ouarzazate has plenty of modern hotels but is much less dramatic than the scenery that surrounds it. The town stands beside a large **artificial lake**, formed by the Barrage el-Mansour (El-Mansour Dam), which holds back the waters of the Oued Drâa.

Kasbah des Glaouis ★★★

Taourirt, on the eastern outskirts of Ouarzazate – about 8km (5 miles) from the centre, was another **stronghold** of the **Glaoui chieftains** of the region and is a spectacular reminder of a turbulent and not-so-distant past. Rectangular walls, almost 500m (1640ft) long, surround a clutter of towers and turrets. Elaborately patterned brickwork adorns the windows, which are guarded by ornate wrought-iron grilles.

Aït Benhaddou ★★★

One of the **finest kasbahs** in Morocco, Aït Benhaddou is situated about 30km (19 miles) northwest of Ouarzazate, on the Marrakech highway. A dramatically located complex of ornamented red stone and mud-brick walls with decorated towers, it stands among green terraces of barley, almond and palm trees, with the High Atlas peaks as a backdrop.

Below: *Aït Benhaddou has been the location for many movies, including Lawrence of Arabia.*

THE DRÂA VALLEY

To the east of Ouarzazate, the highway runs through hill country, climbing the 1692m (5500ft) Tizi-n-Tinififft pass through a bleak but spectacular landscape of shattered, multicoloured rock, and then descends to the small town of **Agdz** (pronounced 'Agadez'), the gateway to the Drâa Valley – a huge, linear oasis formed by the Oued Drâa as it flows through arid, rocky landscapes towards the Sahara.

The river creates a fertile corridor, approximately 200km (125 miles) of irrigated fields, orchards and palmeries in sharp and picturesque contrast to the utterly treeless slopes on either side. Amazingly, the Drâa supports a population of some 800,000 people living in dozens of magnificent kasbahs.

The 95km (60-mile) length of the Drâa Valley between Agdz and Zagora is the most interesting part of the route. **Kasbah villages** not to be missed include **Tamnougalt**, once the capital of the valley; **Igdâoun**, with its strangely shaped towers like flat-topped pyramids; and **Tinezouline**, possibly the most spectacular and one of the most accessible kasbahs.

ZAGORA

The small town of Zagora marks the end of the Drâa Valley, though the river wanders on south and east before crossing into Algeria and the Sahara. Zagora was once an important **caravan terminus** and the homeland of the Saadian dynasty who conquered southern Morocco in the 16th century and eventually ruled an empire that extended across the Sahara desert to Timbuktu. For the visitor, Zagora is mainly important as a place to stop overnight while touring the region.

TAMEGROUTE

Some 18km (11 miles) south of Zagora, Tamegroute is known mainly for its **remarkable mosques** with their conspicuous blue-tiled roofs and brilliant white minarets. The village's fame rests on its importance – since at least the 16th century – as an influential **centre**

MHAMID SOUK

One of the most colourful markets in Morocco takes place every Monday morning at Mhamid, 96km (60 miles) south of Zagora. This village of about 2000 inhabitants is at the end of the road and the beginning of the desert, surrounded by dunes and grim hammada plains. Settlements are thin on the ground and many of the people of the region are **seminomadic pastoralists**, who gather at Mhamid to trade for **essential supplies**. Camels, mules and flocks of sheep abound, driven by Berber herders in striped cotton robes.

Above: *Fortified villages like this one, built of clay bricks strengthened with straw, are typical of the Dadès Valley, between the Atlas Mountains and the Sahara Desert.*
Opposite: *Antiques and curios on display at a roadside stall at Skoura.*

---

of **Islamic learning**, and its Koranic library and religious college are still prestigious. The mosques are closed to visitors.

Librairie Coranique ★

In the centre of the town of Tamegroute, the Koranic Library was founded in the 17th century and houses a remarkable collection of **illuminated Korans**, some of which may be on view; but most are of greater interest to scholars than to the casual visitor. Open 08:00–12:00 and 15:00–17:00, Saturday–Thursday.

Dunes of Tinfou ★

The sand dunes of Tinfou, rising from a stony landscape 5km (3 miles) south of Tamegroute, are the first real indication that you are approaching the verges of the **Sahara**. The clusters of buildings are generally accommodation stopovers and there is no real town here.

THE DADÈS VALLEY

Oued Dadès runs northwest from Ouarzazate, a ribbon of verdure between rugged red hills and cliffs, narrowing some 150km (95 miles) from Ouarzazate into the narrow, awesome **Gorges of the Dadès**. The Oued Dadès, flowing like the Drâa from a source in the High Atlas, waters a chain of oases northeast of Ouarzazate and forms a series of breathtaking gorges and canyons where it cuts through the limestone. Nicknamed the 'valley of a thousand kasbahs', the Dadès is one of the most beautiful regions in Morocco.

Skoura ★

About 42km (26 miles) east of Ouarzazate lies Skoura, the largest of the **oasis** settlements in the valley. It is surrounded by **palmeries** and **kasbah villages**, some of them several centuries old.

Vallée des Roses ★★

Visit the Valley of the Roses, 40km (25 miles) north of the village of El-Kelaâ M'Gouna and 132km (82 miles) north-east of Ouarzazate, in spring when the fields are one huge mass of rose-pink petals. These are used to make **rose-water perfume**, and there is also a picturesque **rose harvest festival** in El-Kelaâ M'Gouna in May.

Dadès Gorge ★★★

A four-wheel-drive vehicle is needed to explore the magnificent **scenery** of the gorge, where the river winds its way through fantastic water-sculpted **rock formations**.

Todra Gorge ★★★

Approximately 15km (9 miles) southeast of the village of Tinerhir, the river passes through the Todra Gorge – nicknamed 'the end of the world' – where two sheer cliffs 300m (985ft) high loom above a river channel only 10m (33ft) wide at its narrowest point. This fantastic **canyon** is one of Morocco's most dramatic sights. Fed by the snows of the High Atlas, the river flowing through it is ice cold, and the sun only strikes the bottom of the gorge before midday. The gorge has its own microclimate, especially at night. Evenings, which can be tropically warm in nearby villages beyond the ends of the gorge, may be bitterly cold within its rock walls. The narrowest sector of the gorge is less than 600m (2000ft) long.

RAIDS AND RALLIES

The famous **Paris–Dakar** and **Atlas** rally contests highlight Morocco's fantastic off-road motoring potential, with thousands of kilometres of challenging desert and mountain tracks. The annual **Friendship Raid** on a route from Tangier to Rabat via the Atlas and the Sahara is a friendly sporting event that attracts young motorcyclists and off-road motorists from all over the world. For information, contact AOI, 67 Rue Nationale, 60800 Crepy en Valois, France, tel: (00 331) 44 59 10 41, fax: (00 331) 44 59 05 76.

THE BLUE SULTAN

In 1912, after the French protectorate over Morocco was announced, the local chieftain **Ahmed el-Hiba** declared himself sultan in Tiznit. Because he and many of his followers wore the blue robes of desert nomads, he was nicknamed the 'Blue Sultan'. With Taroudannt as his base, he made the Sousse the heartland of his revolt, but when he marched on Marrakech, he was defeated by the modern weapons of the French and forced to flee into the deep south, where he died in 1919.

Below: *A well-preserved circuit of battlements and bastions surrounds the town of Taroudannt.*

THE SOUSS VALLEY AND THE ANTI ATLAS

The Oued Souss flows from the slopes of Jebel Toubkal towards the Atlantic in a valley between the High Atlas and the almost equally impressive Anti Atlas. Flowing out of the mountains, the Souss irrigates **fertile plains** before eventually meeting the sea at Agadir. No roads pass through the arid, virtually uninhabited Anti Atlas; excursion coaches bring tourists from Agadir as far south as Guelmin, but there is almost no tourism (and no tourist accommodation) in the region.

Parc National de Souss Massa ★★★

This park with its rich **birdlife** is on the coast, either side of the Oued Massa estuary and 60 km (38 miles) to the south of Agadir. Bald ibis, Bonelli's eagle and many more endemic and migrant species may be seen.

TIN MAL

No more than a shadow of its glorious past clings to Tin Mal, the isolated and partly deserted village that was the birthplace of the **Almohad dynasty**. With the Almohads' conquest of Marrakech in 1147, their

original capital became less important and was gradually abandoned, though it still remained a place of great **religious significance** for the Almohad caliphs and their followers. It was here, too, that the last of the Almohad dynasty made their final stand against the conquering **Merenids**, who captured Tin Mal and sacked its treasures in 1276. The **Mosque of Ibn Toumert**, built in memory of and named after the founder of the Almohad dynasty by his successor, Abd el-Moumen, in 1130, has recently been restored and is well worth seeing.

Tizi-n-Test ★★

At 2092m (6860ft) this dramatic **mountain pass** is one of the highest in the Atlas and you need a good head for heights to appreciate the sometimes dizzying views.

Above: *Tinerhir stands amid vast palm plantations on the fringe of the desert.*

TAROUDANNT

An attractive **Berber town** ringed by mud-brick battlements, with the High Atlas to the north and the Anti Atlas to the south, Taroudannt is more than 1000 years old.

Kasbah ★★

Briefly a capital of the Saadians in the 16th century, Taroudannt has an old kasbah quarter dating from this period. The **small souk** is worth a visit, and you can rent a bicycle or hire a carriage to ride around the extensive **ring of ramparts**.

TIZNIT

The town of Tiznit, some 95km (60 miles) south of Agadir, is much more recent than it appears, for its impressive ring of mud-brick walls was built only in 1881, when **Sultan Moulay al-Hassan** founded it as a **garrison** from which to subdue the Berber clans of the Anti Atlas and the Souss plains.

SKIING THE ATLAS

Morocco offers both downhill and cross-country skiing. In the High Atlas, the resort of **Oukaïmeden**, 70km (43 miles) southeast of Marrakech, offers alpine pistes with lifts and chalets, as does **Mischliffen** in the Middle Atlas, about 50km (30 miles) from Fez. There are also cross-country ski trails in the Rif, the Middle Atlas and the High Atlas. For detailed information, contact the **Royal Moroccan Ski and Mountaineering Federation**, Parc de la Ligue Arabe, BP 15899 Casablanca, tel: (022) 20 37 98, fax: (022) 47 49 79.

Above: *Camels await riders near Zagora in the Drâa Valley.*

The Medina ★★
The **jewellery souk**, off Place al-Machouar in the centre of the old walled town, is worth visiting once the tour coaches from Agadir have left.

Great Mosque ★
Tiznit has an interesting mud-plastered Great Mosque, with strange ledges that jut from its walls – these are used as perches for workmen during the **annual replastering** of the mosque. Similar mosques are found on the other side of the Sahara, in Mali, and the technique may have been brought to Morocco by caravan traders from Timbuktu.

THE DESERT SOUTH
Southern Morocco is a region of barren, gravel desert, semidesert landscapes and vast distances, which explains why it has been little touched by tourism. Most of Western Sahara was annexed by Morocco in 1975 following **Spanish withdrawal** from the region. When Mauritania withdrew its claim on the southern portion in 1979, Morocco annexed that too. **Polisario guerrillas** began raiding Moroccan outposts in Western Sahara in 1976, and in 1982 the **Saharawi Arab Democratic Republic** (SADR) was admitted to the **Organization of African Unity** (OAU). In response, Morocco suspended its membership of the OAU. Most indigenous Saharawi are of **Berber** and **Arab** descent but had a distinctive, semi-nomadic and pastoralist lifestyle similar to the Bedouin of Arabia. Most have been driven into exile, and some 300,000 Saharawi live in refugee camps around Tindouf, in southwestern **Algeria**. With the breakdown of the UN-brokered ceasefire between the two sides in 2001 there is little prospect of their return.

Morocco has encouraged its own people to settle in the region through tax and housing incentives. Most of them are employed in the **phosphate-mining** and fish-processing industries, and Morocco maintains strong military garrisons throughout the region. As a result, most settlements are an unappealing hybrid of armed camp and grimy company town.

GUELMIN

Guelmin (also called Goulimime) is the most visited town in the deep south, once famed for its **camel market**, which attracted traders from the most remote desert oases beyond Morocco's borders. South of here the true desert starts, and Guelmin has throughout its history been an entrepôt for **trans-Saharan trade**. Its Sunday market is the main attraction, and, as Guelmin is within day-trip distance of Agadir, the town panders considerably to tourism – most of the so-called 'blue men' who pose for tourist cameras are not desert nomads at all, but settled locals who dress up in Tuareg robes to earn a little *baksheesh*. But the dusty desert gateway of Guelmin is no longer a terminus for the camel caravans that were its lifeblood, and the true Tuareg have been forced by war and drought to abandon their nomadic lifestyle. The camel market is no more and the 'Tuareg' dancers who perform for visiting coach parties are mostly from Casablanca and Agadir.

THE COAST

The desert coast has some entirely undeveloped stretches of Atlantic sand, but most of its towns are grimy little places, involved mainly in the **phosphate trade** or **trawler fishing**, and are strongly garrisoned by the Moroccan army. Accommodation here is very basic, and due to fishing, canning, and phosphate mining and processing, many of the beaches near the settlements are polluted.

SOUTHERN CONFLICT

National pride obviously played its part in the campaign to wrest the Sahara region from Spain, but King Hassan had more pragmatic reasons too. This apparent desert is more valuable than it appears, with rich phosphate deposits and a long coastline, which gives Morocco control over rich Atlantic fishing grounds. Algeria's tacit support for **Polisario** (see page 26) is due as much to a desire for access to these resources as to real sympathy for the Saharawi cause.

Below: *A blue-robed Berber opts for modern transportation.*

Above: *Brightly painted 'teleboutiques' offer international phone and fax connections even in remote villages in the Drâa Valley.*

Sidi Ifni

Built during the 1930s under the Spanish occupation and then handed back in 1969, Sidi Ifni is a peculiar little town consisting of both **Spanish** and **Moroccan buildings** laid out on a grid pattern, with empty and windswept **beaches** to the north and south.

Tan Tan

Tan Tan is situated some 125km (78 miles) to the southwest of Guelmin, close to the coast, and is a drab **mining and garrison town** with a population of around 50,000. Tan Tan Plage, its port, is an unprepossessing and smelly spot; its main industry is sardine and tuna canning and its beach is unpleasantly polluted with cannery effluent.

Laâyoune and Around

The only reason to venture this far south is to travel onward across the **border** into **Mauritania**. Laâyoune is the most important town in the Western Sahara, with a population of around 125,000 and a strong **military and UN presence**. Surrounded by desert, it has no sights worth seeing. Settlements south of Laâyoune, including Boujdour and Dakhla, have no facilities for tourism, and the hundreds of kilometres of *hammada* – flat, treeless gravel plains – between Laâyoune and the southern border make for very monotonous travelling.

The High Atlas, Anti Atlas and Sahara at a Glance

BEST TIMES TO VISIT

Summer temperatures climb to above 40°C (104°F) in the desert, and High Atlas passes may be blocked by snow in winter. Best times are spring and early summer (Mar–May) and autumn (Oct–Nov. Spring flowers on the steppe fringing the Sahara are spectacular in Mar–Apr.

GETTING THERE

By Air: Flights from Casablanca for domestic flights to Dakhla, Ouarzazate, and Laâyoune.
By Road: Buses from Marrakech to Ouarzazate and Taroudannt, and from Agadir to Tiznit, Guelmin and south.

GETTING AROUND

Grands taxis from Ouarzazate onward into the Drâa and Dadès valleys. **Four-wheel-drive vehicles** recommended for independent travel beyond Ouarzazate and Guelmin.

WHERE TO STAY

The choice is largely between luxury hotels and very cheap and basic guesthouses.

Imlil (Jebel Toubkal)
LUXURY
Kasbah du Toubkal, Route de Toubkal, Imlil, tel: (044) 48 56 11, fax: (044) 48 56 36, www.kasbahdutoubkal.com e-mail: kasbah@discover.ltd.uk Five-bedroomed Berber mansion on the outskirts of the national park. Excellent base for climbing Toubkal.

Taroudannt
LUXURY
La Gazelle d'Or, BP 260, tel: (044) 85 20 39, fax: (044) 85 27 37, www.gazelle.dor.com Lush gardens, pavilions, heated pool, golf course, 8km (5 miles) outside Taroudannt.

Ouarzazate
LUXURY
Le Berbère Palace, Mansour Eddahbi, tel: (044) 88 31 05, fax: (044) 88 36 15, www.ouarzazate.com On a natural site, in original Berber style, attractive furnishings; superb swimming pool.
Hôtel Riad Salam, Boulevard Mohammed V, tel: (044) 88 33 35, fax: (044) 88 27 66. Full of character and charm, built within two traditional kasbahs with a large pool and gardens full of palm trees; has the two top restaurants in Ouarzazate.

Tiznit (Tafraoute)
MID-RANGE
Hôtel Kerdous, Route Tiznit–Tafraoute (54km/34 miles), tel: (044) 86 20 63, fax: (044) 60 03 15. Four-star, fine mountain views, roughly midway between Tiznit and Tafraoute.

Zagora
MID-RANGE
Hôtel-Restaurant Kasbah-Asmaa, Route de la Palmeraie, Amazrou, Zagora, tel: (024) 84 75 99, fax: (044) 84 75 27, www.asmaa-zagora.com Best in Zagora; garden, pool; good restaurant in a nomad tent.

WHERE TO EAT

In most of the region, the best (often only) place to eat is in a hotel. Ouarzazate has a couple of independent restaurants.

TOURS AND EXCURSIONS

For guided ascents of Jebel Toubkal, walks in Jebel Toubkal National Park and other High Atlas treks, contact **Club Alpin Francais**, BP 6178, Casablanca, tel: (022) 27 00 90, www.caf-maroc.com For details of ski slopes and resorts in the High Atlas, contact the **Federation Royale Marocaine de Ski de Montagne**, Parc de la Ligue Arabe, BP 15899, Casablanca, tel: (022) 47 49 79, www.sportail.ma All hotels listed here offer excursions into the desert, mountains and river valleys by four-wheel-drive vehicle or minibus.

DRÂA VALLEY	J	F	M	A	M	J	J	A	S	O	N	D
AVERAGE TEMP. °F	64	66	68	72	77	88	100	100	88	77	70	61
AVERAGE TEMP. °C	18	19	20	22	25	31	38	38	31	25	21	16
HOURS OF SUN DAILY	8	8	9	10	11	11	12	12	12	12	12	8
RAINFALL in	0	0	0.2	0.1	0	0	0	0	0.4	0.3	0.3	0.3
RAINFALL mm	2	1	5	3	1	1	1	1	10	9	8	7
DAYS OF RAINFALL	1	1	1	1	1	1	1	1	3	3	3	3

Travel Tips

Tourist Information

The **Moroccan National Tourist Office (MNTO)** has offices in London, Montreal, New York, Orlando, Sydney, Brussels, Düsseldorf, Jeddah, Lisbon, Madrid, Paris, Milan, Stockholm, Tokyo and Zürich. These provide information, brochures and maps of major cities; lists of tour operators offering package holidays; and lists of hotels, campsites and youth hostels. The Reservations Centre does accommodation bookings and tickets for festivals and events; website: www.tourist-offices.org.uk/Morocco **Head office**: 30 Avenue des FAR, Casablanca, tel: (022) 231 2223, fax: (022) 229 4407. **MNTO International Reservations Centre**: 25 Rue de Foucault, Casablanca, tel: (022) 231 2223, fax: 229 4403.

Entry Requirements

Passports must be valid for at least six months after date of entry. Citizens of EU countries, USA, Australia, Canada and New Zealand do not need visas for stays of less than 90 days. South African and Zimbabwean citizens need visas.

Customs

Duty-free allowances are: 1 bottle of wine and 1 bottle of spirits (or three bottles of wine); 200 cigarettes or 50 cigars or 250g (0.5 lb) of tobacco. There are no published restrictions on perfume. There are usually no restrictions on cameras, video cameras and sports equipment for non-commercial use.

Health Requirements

No immunizations are usually required for entry. Those arriving directly from southern Africa may require proof of immunization against yellow fever. Your doctor may recommend immunization against typhoid, tetanus, hepatitis and meningitis.

Getting There

By Air: Direct scheduled flights to Casablanca and Marrakech from most European capitals. Connections at Casablanca for internal flights to Agadir, Al Hoceima, Dakhla, Fez, Laâyoune, Marrakech, Ouarzazate, Oujda, Rabat-Salé, Tangier and Tetouan. Charter flights operate from several European cities direct to Agadir and Tangier. These are generally sold as part of a package holiday that includes accommodation.

By Road: The land border with Algeria is currently closed and travel to/through Algeria is not advised due to severe security problems. With four-wheel-drive vehicles and proper equipment, experienced drivers can drive through the Western Sahara to Mauritania in West Africa.

By Rail: There are no inter-national rail connections.

By Ferry: Very frequent ferry connections to Tangier, Ceuta and Melilla from Spanish ports, including Algeciras and Almeria, and weekly ferries from Sete in southern France.

What to Pack

Morocco is a conservative Muslim country. Shorts, halter-neck tops and beach-wear are acceptable only in resorts around Tangier and Agadir (and, on women, may attract unwelcome attention and sexual approaches even there). Elsewhere, revealing garments are frowned upon. Light long-sleeved shirts or blouses, long trousers and dresses will not offend, and are also a sensible precaution against the harsh summer sun. In the desert and the High Atlas, nights can be cool or chilly even in summer, and for winter visits warm, waterproof clothing is required – snow is common at high altitudes. Mosquito repellent containing 'deet' (diethyltoluamide) is most effective. Photographers using slide or specialist film should take plenty, as only standard print film is readily available. Sunglasses protect eyes against dust and fierce sun, and a sunhat or baseball cap is also a necessity.

Money Matters

Currency: The Moroccan dirham is divided into 100 centimes. Moroccan currency is not obtainable abroad and may not be exported. Dirham notes are in denominations of 10, 50, 100, and 200. Coins are in denominations of 1 and 5 dirhams and 5, 10, 20 and 50 centimes.

Exchange: US dollars and sterling are readily exchangeable at banks and approved exchange offices where no commission is charged, and at larger hotels. From 2002, the new European Union currency, the Euro, replaces all EU currencies except sterling, Danish krone and Swedish krona, and should be accepted at all banks and exchange offices. Changing money in the street is illegal – and an invitation to be robbed. You can use debit or credit cards to withdraw money from automatic teller

machines in larger towns.

Credit cards: These are generally accepted in shops, more upscale restaurants, major hotels and by souk craftsmen.

Tipping: Small-denomination notes and coins are useful for tipping guides, taxi drivers, gatekeepers and beggars.

Accommodation

Morocco has around 600 **hotels** graded from one to five stars, including some with world-class facilities and style. The most stylish of all are to be found in Marrakech, Fez and Essaouira, and in the High Atlas kasbah villages. Purpose-built resort hotels cluster around Agadir and on the coast near Tangier. International-standard hotels in the Casablanca and Rabat area are pitched at business travellers and conventioneers as well as holidaymakers, and facilities and service standards reflect this mixed clientele. Many larger four- and five-star hotels have excellent golf and tennis facilities. A new phenomenon in Morocco is the **riad**, or traditional town house, converted into up-market bed-and-breakfast accommodation, usually with fewer than 12 rooms. Built around an inner courtyard, these are often colourfully decorated in traditional style, furnished with Moroccan antiques, and offer excellent value for money. A few even have pools. Most riads are found in Marrakech, with some in Essaouira and Fez. There are also around 1000 smaller unclassified hotels, most of

which are very basic and can be dirty and noisy too. There are 87 official **camping and caravan sites** in Morocco, most in scenic locations in the mountains, at oases and on the beach. These are extremely cheap. Facilities vary but are usually unsophisticated. Full list available from MNTO offices. MNTO offices also have lists of **youth hostels** and **rest centres** for tourists under 30, and of **mountain refuges** for hikers in the Atlas mountains and national parks.

Eating Out

Tangier, Casablanca, Rabat, Essaouira, Marrakech and Fez have truly excellent Moroccan and international restaurants. Most of the best international eateries are within major hotels, but there are many superb independent restaurants serving the finest Moroccan cuisine. Essaouira, on the Atlantic coast, and Ksar es Seghir, on the Mediterranean, have noteworthy seafood. Agadir, which attracts a multinational, mainly European clientele of package holidaymakers, has a host of generic pizza, pasta, burger and grill restaurants pandering to northern tastes. In many other places, the food may be almost as good, but is more likely to be found in smaller, simpler eating places – and even on street stands such as those that sell delicious fresh sardines on the quayside at Essaouira, where there is no fixed menu and you can choose from what is available by visiting the kitchen. The price range is as wide as the choice of eating places – in Marrakech's most prestigious hotel, La Mamounia, dinner will be no cheaper than in London or Paris, while in a small restaurant, it can be almost ridiculously cheap. In this devoutly Muslim country, many simpler eating places do not serve alcohol, especially those within the old medina of each city, close to the main mosques; if you want wine with dinner, head for a restaurant in the new town.

Transport

By Air: Royal Air Maroc flies from Casablanca to Agadir, Al Hoceima, Dakhla, Laâyoune, Fez, Marrakech, Ouarzazate, Oujda, Rabat-Salé, Smara, Tangier, Tan Tan and Tetouan. **By Road:** Roads are generally good, and all but 1500km (930 miles) of Morocco's 11,000km (6800 miles) of main road is paved. An Atlantic coast motorway links Casablanca with Rabat and north as far as Kenitra and is being extended to Tangier. **Road signs** are in French and Arabic, and the **speed limit** is 120kph (76mph) on motorways, 100kph (60mph) on main roads, 40–60kph (25–40mph) in towns. Traffic is undisciplined; drive defensively and beware of unexpected hazards such as goats, donkeys and even (in the south) camels. For renting a car, international chains' **car-hire** agencies are preferable to local companies. Four-wheel-drive vehicles are needed for desert travel and recommended for the Atlas in winter. On desert tracks and other difficult terrain, do not drive alone; wait for other vehicles and drive in convoy. Long distance, air-conditioned **buses** are the favoured mode of transport for most Moroccans. The main long-distance bus company, CTM, has a nationwide network. There are intercity bus stations in all Moroccan cities and large towns (often next to the railway station). Timetables and route information from MNTO offices and from **CTM**, 23 Rue Leon l'Africain, Casablanca, tel: (022) 244 8127, fax: (022) 231 7406.

Grands taxis (big taxis) are shared long-distance taxis running between towns on more-or-less fixed routes and carry a maximum of six people. They can be a useful alternative if you don't want to wait for a scheduled bus or are heading off the main bus routes. Agree the fare before setting off. *Grands taxis* usually wait for passengers at rail stations and bus stations.

Business Hours

Unlike many Muslim countries, Morocco has a Monday–Friday, European-style working week. Friday, the holiest day of the Muslim week, is not an official day off, but public- and private-sector companies allow their employees an extended Friday lunch break to attend midday prayers.

Government offices are open 08:30–12:00 and 14:00–18:30 Monday–Thursday, 08:30–11:30 and 15:00–18:30 Friday. **Banks and commercial offices** open 08:15–11:30 and 14:15–16:00 Monday–Friday; June, July, August: 08:00–15:00 Monday–Friday; during the Holy Month of Ramadan: 09:30–14:00 Monday–Friday. Bank counters at airports usually stay open until the last arrival/departure of the day.

Shops are usually open 08:00–12:30 and 14:30–18:30, and food shops even longer. In the medina, usually the traditionally minded heart of each town, most shops close Friday, Saturday and Sunday.

Time Difference

Morocco is on GMT.

From	To	Multiply By
	CONVERSION CHART	
Millimetres	Inches	0.0394
Metres	Yards	1.0936
Metres	Feet	3.281
Kilometres	Miles	0.6214
Square kilometres	Square miles	0.386
Hectares	Acres	2.471
Litres	Pints	1.760
Kilograms	Pounds	2.205
Tonnes	Tons	0.984
To convert Celsius to Fahrenheit: x 9 ÷ 5 + 32		

Communications

Telephone boxes are widespread and take coins and cards, which can be bought in post offices and at some cigarette stores and kiosks (*tabacs*). You can also call from telephone boxes inside post offices, paying at a counter at the end of the call. Telephone enquiries (domestic), tel: 15, and international enquiries, tel: 12. Most hotels load their phone charges and/or impose a minimum charge that can make even a short call very expensive. The international dialling code for Morocco is 00 212.

Post offices open 08:30–11:45 and 14:30–18:30 Monday–Friday. Main post offices are: **Agadir**, corner Avenue du Prince Moulay Abdallah and Avenue Sidi Mohammed; telephone office open 08:00–21:00 daily. **Casablanca**, corner Boulevard de Paris and Avenue Hassan II; 24-hour (daily) international telephone office entrance on Boulevard de Paris. **Fez**, corner Avenue Hassan II and Boulevard Mohammed V; international telephone office entrance on Boulevard Mohammed V, open 08:30–21:00 Monday–Friday. **Marrakech**, Place du 16 Novembre; telephone office open 08:30–21:00 (daily). **Rabat**, corner Rue Soekarno and Avenue Mohammed V; 24-hour (daily) telephone office. **Tangier** main post office, corner Rue de Belgique and Rue de Fez; telephone office open 08:30–12:15 and 14:30–18:45 daily.

Electricity

220V AC in newer buildings, 110V in most places in the medina and smaller towns and villages. Plugs are European-style two-pin.

Weights and Measures

Metric system is in operation.

Health Precautions

No obligatory immunizations, but seek medical advice on **immunization** against hepatitis, meningitis, tetanus and typhoid. Use insect repellent against **mosquitoes**. Avoid drinking **tap water**. Bottled water is available everywhere. Beware of **sunburn** and use high-factor sunblock. In the deep south and the oases, beware of **heat exhaustion**. Wear a hat, and drink plenty of water.

Health Services

Private health care is expensive and limited; outside the major cities, there are few private hospitals offering the full spectrum of services. Comprehensive **medical insurance**, including emergency repatriation costs, is essential.

Personal Safety

Generally, Morocco is safe in terms of crime. Violent crime against foreigners is rare, but **petty theft** is not unusual and basic precautions should be observed. Walking after dark in the older parts of town (and in less central parts of new town districts) is ill-advised. Watch your belongings, especially on buses and trains. Do not leave valuables in your room. Carry money, tickets,

USEFUL WORDS AND PHRASES

Hello • La-bas/salaam aleikum
Good morning • *Saba el-kher*
Good evening • *Masa el-kher*
Please (to a man) • *Afaq*
Please (to a woman) • *Afiq*
Thank you • *Shoqran*
Yes • *Iyeh*
No • *La*
Where • *Fein*
Bus • *Al-kar*
Train • *Al-qitar*
Bank • *Al-banqa*
Market • *As-souq*
Post office • *Al-bosta*
Hotel • *Al-otel*

Days of the Week
Monday • *Al-itnen*
Tuesday • *Al-talata*
Wednesday • *Al-arba*
Thursday • *Al-khamis*
Friday • *Al-juma*
Saturday • *As-sabt*
Sunday • *Al-ahad*

Numbers
Zero • *Sifr*
One • *Wahid*
Two • *Itnin*
Three • *Talata*
Four • *Arbaa*
Five • *Khamsa*
Six • *Sitta*
Seven • *Saba'a*
Eight • *Tamanya*
Nine • *Tissa*
Ten • *Ashara*
Twenty • *'Ashreen*
Thirty • *Talateen*
Fourty • *Araba'een*
Fifty • *Khamseen*
Sixty • *Sitteen*
Seventy • *Saba'een*
Eighty • *Tamaneen*
Ninety • *Tissaeen*
One hundred • *Miyya*
One thousand • *Alf*

PUBLIC HOLIDAYS

1 January • New Year's Day
11 January • Proclamation of
Independence Day
3 March • Throne Day
1 May • May (Workers') Day
23 May • National Day
9 July • Young People's Day
14 August • Wadi
Eddahab Day
20 August • King's and
People's Revolution Day
6 November • Green
March Day
18 November •
Independence Day

passport and credit cards in a concealed wallet or inner pocket, not in a 'bum-bag', 'moon-bag' or shoulder bag. **Hashish** and **kif** are widely used and sold in Morocco and (especially in Marrakech, Essaouira and Chefchaouen) street dealers may try to sell you small amounts. In Ketama, centre of the Rif hashish trade, they may try to sell you large amounts. Be aware that, though widely used, drugs are illegal in Morocco and Moroccan prisons are very unpleasant.

Emergencies
Police, tel: 19; **ambulance** and **fire service**, tel: 15; **highway emergencies**, tel: 177. Do not count on any of these speaking English, but they speak French.

Etiquette
Wearing skimpy clothes (shorts and singlets) away from the beach (even on it) may offend conservative Moroccans – you often see Moroccan women sitting on the beach clad from

neck to ankle in *djellaba*. Public displays of affection between the sexes are rare – rarer, in fact, than between men, who often embrace when meeting and hold hands when walking. Remove shoes when entering a private home. Alcohol is unlikely to be available in most medina restaurants and cafés (except in the more secluded places out of sight of censorious locals), but can be found in many hotels and restaurants in the newer part of town. It is rude to photograph people without permission and you should not even be seen to point a camera at government buildings, military installations or even civil airports.

Language
Classical Arabic is the official language. The Moroccan **dialect** form of Arabic is in everyday use, along with the Berber dialects spoken in the Rif, the Atlas and the Souss. Most Moroccans involved in tourism speak fluent **French**, along with some **English**.

Holidays and Festivals
Morocco uses the Gregorian calendar but Muslim religious days are calculated according to the Islamic calendar, which has 12 lunar months and a year that is 11 days shorter, so feast days arrive 10–12 days earlier each year. As they depend on the first sighting of the new moon, exact dates cannot be predicted far in advance. All Muslim religious holidays are public holidays.

Festivities and Moussems
Morocco has local festivities that may well pre-date Islam and mark the seasons and harvests of each region. There are also *moussems*, gatherings to pay homage to respected holy men. Dances, processions, feasting, exhibitions of horsemanship and the wearing of traditional costume are part of these often spectacular events. Dates depend on the lunar calendar and local conditions, but can usually be given by local offices of the MNTO.

GOOD READING

Bowles, Paul (1985) *Their Heads are Green and Their Hands are Blue* (Peter Owen).
Canetti, Elias (1978) *The Voices of Marrakech* (Marion Boyars).
Choukri, Mohammed (1987) *For Bread Alone*, translated by Paul Bowles (Grafton).
Finlayson, Iain (1992) *Tangier: City of the Dream* (Flamingo).
Freud, Emma (1996) *Hideous Kinky* (Penguin).
Maalouf, Amin (1994) *Leo the African* (Abacus).
Mackintosh-Smith, Tim (2001) *Travels with a Tangerine* (John Murray).
Matthews, Patrick (2001) *Cannabis Culture* (Bloomsbury).
Maxwell, Gavin (1966) *Lords of the Atlas* (Longmans Green).
The Magic of Morocco (various photographers, Vilo, 2001).